Montana Chillers

13 True Tales of Ghosts and Hauntings

by

Ellen Baumler

illustrations by Robert Rath

FARCOUNTRY PRESS

ISBN 10: 1-56037-496-9
ISBN 13: 978-1-56037-496-1

© 2009 by Farcountry Press
Text © 2009 by Ellen Baumler
Illustrations © 2009 by Farcountry Press

For more information on our books, write Farcountry Press, P.O. Box 5630, Helena, MT 59604; call (800) 821-3874; or visit www.farcountrypress.com.

Library of Congress Cataloging-in-Publication Data

Baumler, Ellen.
  Montana chillers : 13 true tales of ghosts and hauntings / Ellen Baumler.
     p. cm.
  ISBN-13: 978-1-56037-496-1
  ISBN-10: 1-56037-496-9
  1. Ghosts--Montana. 2. Haunted places--Montana. I. Title.
  BF1472.U6B378 2009
  133.109786--dc22
                              2009026322

 Produced and printed in the United States of America.

18   17   16   15   14   2   3   4   5   6

Table of Contents

Introduction

What Are Ghosts?

Most people believe that *ghosts*—also called *spirits* or *apparitions*—are the souls of people or animals who have died. Ghosts that appear in the world of the living, some people say, are souls that have become stuck here, unable to move into the afterlife.

Although no one can say for certain whether ghosts exist, people have believed in them since the very beginning of time. Many people, maybe even you, claim to have seen ghosts.

Some people laugh at those who believe they have experienced the *supernatural,* which is anything that goes beyond scientific understanding. Those who make fun are the ones who need proof. When something happens to you that you cannot explain, you know it happened. You do not need convincing.

Ghost sightings and other supernatural events happen only by chance. For example, you can never predict when, or if, a ghost is going to appear. You never know when you might hear phantom footsteps or feel an electricity in the air that makes your skin prickle. If we could call these things up whenever we wanted to, there would be no mystery.

Playback, Active Spirits, and Dreams

When we think about ghosts and the supernatural, we imagine misty figures walking through dark hallways. But people experience the supernatural in different ways. There seem to be three main kinds of experiences: "playback," encounters with active spirits, and dreams.

Playback

The most common supernatural experience is *"playback."* A playback can be something you see, hear, or even smell. But what is it?

Living things are made of energy that never goes away. When a living thing dies, what happens to its energy? No one knows for sure. Some people think that after a person or animal dies, his or her energy remains like a memory. For example, if you see someone in a window, as in "Mystery of the Metal Coffin" on page 112, it is probably a playback, a memory of someone who stood in that place many times during life. When the person died, the memory remained and sometimes reveals itself so that others can see it.

When people experience this leftover energy, it is almost like walking into a kind of time warp. Something that happened in the past happens over and over again. It is like watching a scene in a play.

The Butte–Silver Bow County Public Archives is one place where people have experienced playback. The building was originally the Quartz Street Fire Station, built in 1900. Butte had many terrible fires and mining disasters. The fire station saw plenty of action. Imagine the fire alarms sounding and the men rushing to put on their gear. Time after time until the station closed, firemen rushed to answer the alarms. All that energy and nervous anticipation the men must have felt each time the alarms sounded seems to have remained in the building.

Today the building is no longer a fire station. It is a place for storing county records. People who work there have seen and heard some creepy things. When night falls and the building is empty, late-night visitors report that they can hear the firemen murmuring in the dark. Disconnected alarm bells sometimes clang. Several photographs taken at night inside the building show an odd mist. This gathering of energy into a misty, formless mass that shows up in photographs and videos is called *ectoplasm*. You cannot usually see it with your eyes. Paranormal investigators also call ectoplasm *ghost mist, ghost fog,* or *ghost vapors.*

It's important to remember that the figures or sounds that are sometimes associated with playback don't want anything from you, and they don't interact with you. Their energy just materializes sometimes so that you can see them, hear them, smell them, or sense that they are there.

If you want to read more about playback, check out these

Misty ectoplasm appears in this photograph taken by ghost hunters inside the old state prison in Deer Lodge. PHOTO COURTESY OF JULIA BREWER.

stories in the book: "Haunted Bannack" (page 64) and "The Weeping Woman of Fish Creek" (page 98).

Active Spirits

An active spirit is a person or an animal who has died and is stuck in the world of the living. Seeing an active spirit is the rarest kind of supernatural experience. In these cases, ghost experts believe that the spirit may want you to see it because it may have a message to give you or want you to do some task for it.

Joyce Walker lives in south-central Montana and loves the outdoors. She came upon an active spirit once a few years ago when she was hunting with her dad. Joyce and her dad had permission to hunt on a private ranch in Jefferson County. Livestock was sometimes pastured there, but the rancher had moved the animals elsewhere to keep them safe during hunting season. There was a lean-to in this pasture. It was open on all four sides, with a roof that gave the animals a little shelter from the hot sun and the rain.

Joyce was standing near the lean-to with her eye on the bushes at the edge of the pasture. Her dad was back at the car. She clearly heard the sound of a horse stomping his hooves behind her. She could hear his snorts and the swish of his tail. She whirled around. Nothing was there.

Joyce ran to her dad and told him what had happened. They both went back to the lean-to and began to walk around it. On the other side of the little shelter, they found the skeleton of a horse.

"It was as if the horse had died," Joyce explained, "and no one knew what happened to him. I think he wanted me to find him so someone would know that he was there, so that he could be at peace."

Active spirits in this book include Mrs. Elling in "The Ghost of Elling House" (page 38) and Mr. Davey in "Garnet Ghost Town" (page 56).

A *poltergeist* is a kind of active spirit that you can't see—but you can see the result of what it does. Poltergeists are mischievous spirits that make noise, move objects, play tricks, and generally bother those they target. What happens in "The Harlem Hotel" (page 18) may be the result of a poltergeist.

Dreams

A third kind of supernatural experience may come not from ghosts but from the state of dreaming.

Sylvia Browne, who is a famous psychic, tells a story about a woman who had very vivid dreams. She dreamed about a cottage, time after time. She knew every piece of furniture and every nook and cranny of the house. Finally, the dreams were so distressing that she got on the Internet and found the address. She went there and boldly knocked on the door. The owners answered the door, and when they saw her, they gasped.

"Oh!" they cried. "You are our ghost!"

The woman had had such vivid dreams of the house that the homeowners could see her essence wandering through the rooms. They thought she was a ghost.

Some believe this explains how sometimes, when you think you see a ghost, you might be seeing someone who is dreaming. Experts call this *teleportation*, transporting yourself to a place where your physical body is not. The person is not really a ghost and is not dead at all. Teleportation through dreaming is one explanation for the sightings of the little boy in "The Legend of the Boy Who Drowned" (page 32).

Ghost Hunters

Some people don't just wait around for a ghost to find *them*. They go out looking for ghosts. Professional *ghost hunters* are always searching for evidence of the supernatural. They work to track down ghosts and try to find evidence that they exist.

Ghost hunters investigate places that might be haunted. In order to detect supernatural activity, ghost hunters use special equipment. Some believe that when ghosts are trying to appear, they gather energy around them. This changes the temperature of the air, creating *hot spots* or *cold spots*. Ghost hunters use *infrared thermometers* and *digital thermometers* to measure these changes. A sudden drop or rise in temperature of 10 degrees or more is considered a paranormal reading.

Ghost hunters listen for electronic voice phenomena (EVPs) using highly sensitive digital recorders. EVPs are unexplained recorded sounds. You can't hear them when they are happening

—only when you play back the recording. During an investigation, ghost hunters place recorders around a room and ask questions such as "Is anyone there?" or "Do you have something you would like to tell us?" Then they listen to the recordings later, to see what happened. The recorders sometimes pick up sounds like footsteps, rapping, doors creaking, and, on rare occasions, words or phrases.

The Old Montana State Prison Museum in Deer Lodge is a favorite place for ghost hunters and is known for its supernatural activity. During one investigation, ghost hunters let their recorders run for several hours in the maximum-security area. Later, they listened to the recordings. They captured what they believe to be several EVPs. One of these came in answer to the investigator's question "Is anyone there?" A voice distinctly said, "You can't see me." Other types of EVPs captured at the prison during investigations include the clanging of the cell doors and the sounds of heavy footsteps.

Motion sensors are another electronic device useful to ghost hunters. They use these devices to capture the possible movement of energy you can't see with your eyes.

Ghostly Evidence

You don't have to be a ghost hunter to come face to face with the unexplained. Ordinary people sometimes find mysterious images in photographs. They see ghostly apparitions. Or they experience the supernatural through smells, noises, or feelings. And sometimes, you can look to the past for evidence.

Photographs

It is rare, but sometimes cameras capture strange images that cannot be explained. The staff of the Montana Heritage Commission, who takes care of the buildings at Virginia City and Nevada City, snapped a photo in Nevada City that gave everyone chills. A few years ago, some of the commission staff gathered at the place where a man named George Ives was hanged for murder on December 21, 1863. The date was December 21, 2006, the 143rd anniversary of Ives' death. The staff thought it would be fun to take a photo of the site just after sunset, at about the time of day the hanging took place so long ago. They saw nothing unusual when they took the picture.

Later, when they downloaded the photo onto a computer, they were astonished to see the profile of a man. Historians know what Ives looked like. The man was not Ives. No one on the staff recognized him. Could the image be of someone who witnessed Ives' hanging back in 1863?

Take a look at some of the other photographs in this book. What do you see?

Orbs

Some people believe that orbs are the souls of people who have passed on. They usually travel in groups. Orbs appear as round spots that sometimes appear in photographs (see pages 14 and 73). The people taking the photographs don't see them when they snap the picture—only later do they spot these startling shapes.

George Ives swung from the gallows on this spot in Nevada City in 1863. This photograph, taken on the 143rd anniversary of his hanging, captured the strange image of an unidentified man. PHOTO BY BILL PETERSON, MONTANA HERITAGE COMMISSION.

Orbs appear in this photo taken in the sitting room of the Daly Mansion in Hamilton.
PHOTO COURTESY OF TORTURED SOULS INVESTIGATIONS, WWW.TSIMT.NET.

Some orbs are solid, and some are clear. Orbs occasionally have a colored center or bands of color inside them. Sometimes these shapes are just dirt, dust particles, moisture, or even bugs. But sometimes, there is no such explanation. Maybe you have taken pictures that have orbs.

Study the Past

While ghost hunters search for physical evidence, some historians search for past events that might explain why a supernatural event occurred. Ghost hunters often forget to wonder *why* a supernatural event has happened. The *why* is just as important as the physical evidence.

Consider the old building near the historic train depot in Billings. It served many purposes in its long life. For a while in the 1980s, it was a dinner theater. During this time, mirrors lined one side of the stage. Actors on stage would sometimes look in the mirror and see a soldier there, standing next to the audience. As they shifted their gaze between the mirror and the audience, the actors realized the soldier's image appeared only in the mirror!

Why would the ghost of a soldier haunt this building? Research shows that, in 1945, the building was the headquarters for a chain of grocery stores. The basement had a huge refrigerated warehouse. One December night during a terrible blizzard, a military plane crashed into a nearby neighborhood. The pilot, copilot, and seventeen soldiers died. No funeral home in Billings had space to store that many bodies. Authorities put thirteen of the victims in the refrigerated basement of the grocery warehouse to await identification. Perhaps the ghostly soldier is a playback of one of those young men.

The story of the Billings warehouse shows how important it is to study the past in searching for evidence of ghosts. Physical evidence, like that collected by ghost hunters in pictures, recordings, and temperature readings, is surely interesting. It makes sense, however, to look for the *reason* behind the ghostly activity. You are more likely to find a reason behind a haunting than you are to find physical evidence of it.

Another Kind of Evidence

You may never see a ghost, but that does not mean you will never have a "spirited" encounter. *Seeing* is not the only way to experience the supernatural. Many people have tiny little encounters.

"Spirit tailings," these little chance encounters, fill our everyday lives. Tailings, as you will learn in "Tommyknockers" (page 46), are the piles of dirt miners have thrown away. Spirit tailings, on the other hand, are little hints that the supernatural is all around us. Moved or hidden objects, noises or smells that seem to come from nowhere, and little gifts such as pennies, buttons, and marbles that you might find in odd places are all spirit tailings, reminding us that the past is always with us.

We all search for proof, and maybe some day someone—perhaps you!—will unlock the secrets of the supernatural. When that day comes, however, the mystery will be gone. What makes ghost stories so much fun is that they leave you wondering about what is possible.

Haunted Montana

Montana, as you will discover, has many haunted places. The thirteen *Chillers* collected in this book are about many different places and different kinds of experiences. From "Spirit Horse" (page 24), about a winner who fulfilled a prophesy, to the marbles in "Secrets of the Montana Club" (page 74), the stories are all about real people, real places, and real events. As you read the stories, remember that many people are sharing their personal experiences with you.

While ghost hunters try to physically explain the science behind haunted places, this book instead explains haunted places through the events of the past. Looking at the history behind the haunting, why the person has not moved on, or what message an apparition might be trying to get across is another way to study ghosts.

Keep an open mind, and when you have finished, ask yourself this question: "Do I believe in ghosts?" You might be surprised at your answer.

Story Locations

1. The Harlem Hotel
2. Spirit Horse
3. The Legend of the Boy Who Drowned
4. The Ghost of Elling House
5. Tommyknockers
6. Garnet Ghost Town
7. Haunted Bannack
8. Secrets of the Montana Club
9. The Conrad Mansion
10. The Mansion's Little Ghost
11. The Weeping Woman of Fish Creek
12. Man in the Mirror
13. Mystery of the Metal Coffin

PARENTS HAVE RULES FOR A REASON. BUT SOMETIMES KIDS disobey. Ten-year-old Jeff Bickenheuser had the scare of his life one evening when he broke the rules.

Jeff grew up in the town of Harlem, halfway between Malta and Havre. Harlem sits along Montana's Hi-Line, at the very edge of the Fort Belknap Indian Reservation. Founded in 1889 (the year Montana became a state), Harlem was a railroad town.

The old buildings from Harlem's early days stood empty down by the railroad tracks. Parents warned their children not to play there. The ramshackle buildings were unstable and dangerous.

One summer evening, Jeff and his friend Jesse decided to ignore the rules. They had finished their dinner, and there was still plenty of daylight. The boys headed down to the tracks. They wanted to explore.

The Harlem Hotel was one of the oldest buildings in town. In the early days, it was the finest place to stay in northern Montana. Travelers passing through town spent the night there while waiting for the next train. Ranchers came to do business there. The Harlem Hotel had steam heat and hot water, as well as a fancy dining room. Back in those days, a room cost two dollars a night.

Those days were over. The hotel was abandoned and crumbling, and Jeff and Jesse could hardly imagine that anyone had ever stayed there. It was nothing like the modern motels they'd seen while on vacation. This old hotel was a mess. And that's what they liked. They found the collapsing ruin irresistible.

Sometimes the setting sun casts a bright-red glow as it drops toward the horizon. And that's what the sunset looked like on that warm summer evening. The boys figured they had enough time to explore before it got dark. They imagined there were treasures left from long ago, waiting to be discovered.

Jeff and Jesse made their way to the front door and stepped inside, leaving the heat of the day behind them. The air inside was cool and stale. Light came through the cracks in the walls, casting dim shadows in the old lobby. Dust and cobwebs glistened in the sun's red rays. Shreds of wallpaper clung to the ceiling, and debris littered the floorboards. It was creepy.

The boys stepped out of the lobby and into the dining room, where a hundred years ago guests ate fine meals of roast chicken

or beefsteak, biscuits and honey, and warm apple pie. Through the filtered light, they saw bits of plaster, broken glass, and pigeon droppings covering the floor. Dust hung thick in the air, and cobwebs, fixed to the ceiling, floated above their heads. Although the floor creaked, the building seemed solid enough to the boys. So they carefully climbed the narrow stairway to the second floor. There they found a long, dark hallway.

Jeff wished he had brought his flashlight. He and Jesse moved down the black corridor.

"Hey, Jeff, there's nothing much in this old place," Jesse noted uneasily.

Not wanting his friend to guess that he, too, was a little nervous, Jeff replied gruffly, "Awww. This place is just a dump. But maybe we can find something useful. C'mon. Let's look."

They discovered rooms on each side of the hall and began to peer through each doorway, one by one. There was not much to capture their interest. There was a broken dresser in one room, some rusty bedsprings in another, and a cast-off chair here and there. The boys did not find the treasure they sought.

Jeff and Jesse slowly inched their way to the very last room. As they peered inside, they saw that it was not empty. Sitting in the center was an old-fashioned wooden wheelchair, the kind with a woven seat. They had seen these old wheelchairs in movies, but they had never seen a real one. They knew exactly what it was.

The boys looked at each other, and silently they wondered what it was doing there. They both stood in the doorway for a long moment, staring. The day's last light shone through the

broken window and cast a reddish glow on the solitary object in the middle of the room.

Suddenly, the boys saw something. They looked at each other. Neither said a word, but each knew that the other had seen it.

As the dim light hit the wheelchair, it caught the metal spokes. The boys' eyes grew wide and their mouths hung open as they saw the spokes of the wheels move. Jeff and Jesse froze. In the darkening room, they could see that the wheelchair was creeping toward them.

The boys looked at each other one more time. They both had the same idea. The frightened pair spun around and bounded down the hallway, past all the rooms where darkness now was beginning to creep. Just minutes before, the distance to the stairway had not seemed long at all. Now it seemed endless. They could not get there fast enough.

As they approached the staircase, the only sound was the pounding of their sneakers on the old floorboards and the thumping of their hearts. They could sense something behind them, but neither had the courage to turn around and look.

Finally, after what seemed like an eternity, the pair tumbled down the stairs, one on top of the other, in their rush to get out. They landed at the bottom of the steps in a tangle, picked themselves up, and leapt for the door.

The terrified boys stumbled outside. Only then did Jeff have the courage to turn and look back into the silent building. The doorway to the old hotel, so enticing before, now seemed like a giant mouth that threatened to swallow them. Jeff felt lucky to have escaped.

Out of breath and shaking with fear, Jeff slowly stepped toward the doorway and peered inside. His eyes adjusted to the dark, and he shifted his gaze to the bottom of the stairs, where he and Jesse had been just seconds before. What he saw still sends chills through his body. The memory of it brings on bad dreams, even though he is now an adult. There, at the foot of the stairs, was the empty wheelchair, waiting.

Chapter Two

Spirit Horse

IN THE SHADOW OF THE TOBACCO ROOT MOUNTAINS, just off the highway north of Twin Bridges, sits an unusual barn. Three stories tall, it looks like a giant, red wedding cake. Each layer is a little smaller than the one below it. What's more unusual than how the famous Doncaster Round Barn looks is what happened there.

The story begins far away and over the mountains, where the town of Spokane, Washington, is today. In this place above the Spokane River in 1858, there was a battle between the U.S. Army and the Palouse Indians who lived there. During the clash, Colonel George Wright took 800 horses belonging to a Palouse leader named Tilcoax. When the fighting was over, Colonel Wright had to decide what to do with these horses.

He knew that horses meant everything to the Indians. The tribes used them for transportation, for sport, and as money in trade. These horses were wild and beautiful, and there were many mares and young colts in the herd.

Colonel Wright knew that if he let the horses go, the Indians would take them back. That would never do. He could not keep them because they were too wild for his men to ride. It was a crime on the frontier to kill horses, but this was wartime and Colonel Wright decided that was the only thing to do.

The colonel ordered his soldiers to separate the little colts from their mothers. Next, he ordered his men to club all the little colts to death. Then Colonel Wright ordered the men to shoot all the mares and stallions. It took several days for the soldiers, many of them with tears in their eyes, to carry out these terrible orders. When they finally finished, blood soaked the ground.

The beautiful, spirited wild horses that once raced free in the grassy hills lay dead on the battlefield. A Palouse Indian warrior lay among them. Wounded a few days before in the battle, he had been overlooked by the soldiers. As he lay half-conscious on the bloody ground, he heard the Great Spirit say to him:

> You see all these fine horses with their graceful necks and keen limbs spread on the ground? All is not lost, for one day a spirit horse will return with all the speed, endurance, strength, and fire of these wild horses that lie dead around you.

Their souls will enter into the body of one little
colt, and that colt will accomplish the impossible,
and his name shall be Spokane.

The warrior survived and shared his story. The Indians
grieved over the loss of the horses and their homeland. White
settlers began to pour into the region and farm the lands. People
called the place where this terrible event happened Wright's
Boneyard. It is remembered today as Horse Slaughter Camp.

More than twenty-five years passed after the terrible killing
of the Palouse Indians' wild and beautiful horses. Then, across
the Rocky Mountains in Montana, a settler named Noah
Armstrong bought a farm near Twin Bridges. Noah was in
charge of the Glendale silver mines. Mining had made him a
wealthy man. Noah believed that Montana was the perfect place
to raise thoroughbred horses for racing. He knew that the wild,
rich bunch-grass would make his horses healthy. And he knew
that Montana's high altitude would make their lungs strong for
racing long distances. Noah named his place Doncaster Farm
after Doncaster, one of his favorite racehorses.

Noah built a grand, three-story, round barn with a quarter-
mile track on the ground floor for training his horses. The horses
could train in even the coldest winter weather. The second story
was for storing hay and feed. On the third floor, there was a
water tank. A windmill on the top pumped the water for use on
the ground floor.

In Illinois, Noah bought a lovely horse named Interpose.
Interpose had a colt named Madelin and was also expecting a

foal. Noah brought the pregnant Interpose and baby Madelin to Montana, where he could take good care of them.

Some time later, Noah took a business trip across the Rocky Mountains to the new town of Spokane Falls, Washington. The citizens of Spokane were very generous to Noah and treated him very well. The city's wonderful hospitality greatly impressed Noah. After he had been there for a few days, Noah received a telegram that a fine little foal had been born to Interpose. He liked the town so well that he decided to name the new little foal Spokane.

Months passed, and Spokane grew strong at the Doncaster Farm. He was a small horse and did not appear to be as powerful as some racehorses, but he was sleek and beautiful. His coat was the color of the copper that came out of the mines in Montana. Spokane thrived on Montana's bunch-grass and the high mountain air. Noah's trainer began to work with Spokane in the round barn's quarter-mile track. He discovered that Spokane could run like the wind.

When Spokane was two years old, Noah sent him to Tennessee for more training. Spokane won several races, but no one paid much attention to the little copper-colored horse from Montana. Then when Spokane was three years old, in 1889, the same year that Montana became the forty-first state, Noah Armstrong decided to enter Spokane in the great race, which was run at a racetrack named Churchill Downs. This race is still one of the most important horse races in the United States. Noah was taking a huge gamble on Spokane.

There were eight horses racing in the Kentucky Derby that year. Their names were Cassius, Once Again, Sportsman,

Bootmaker, Hindoocraft, Outbound, Spokane, and Proctor Knott. Everyone thought that the mighty Proctor Knott would win. He was a huge horse, and very powerful, and he had already won some important races for his owner. Not only that, but he was also a Kentucky horse, named for one of the state's governors, and the crowd—most of them Kentuckians—loved him. When he trotted out into view, the crowd cheered wildly. As the eight horses lined up at the starting gate, the crowd made fun of Spokane. People laughed at his small size and expected him to finish last.

At the signal, the red flag went down. The horses were off. The crowd cheered for Proctor Knott as he easily pulled into the lead. He was running hard. As the horses raced around the big track at Churchill Downs, Proctor Knott remained in the lead, followed by Hindoocraft and Bootmaker.

Then something magical happened. Spokane began to pass the other horses. One by one, the others fell behind. He moved from fifth place to third, and then the distance between the little copper-colored Montana horse and the mighty Proctor Knott began to close.

Then Spokane was right behind Proctor Knott. The champion was running too hard; he began to tire. At the finish line, Spokane pulled ahead of Proctor Knott to a breathtaking finish. There were 25,000 people in the grandstands that day, and for years afterward, people talked about this race. It seemed that Spokane ran as if he were on fire, as if some unseen spirit pushed him ahead and gave him wings. Never had anyone seen such a race.

Spokane's record finish of two minutes, thirty-four-and-a-half seconds around the mile-and-a-half track can never be broken. In

1896, the track was shortened to a mile-and-a-quarter length. So Spokane's unbeaten record finish will always stand.

Soon after the race, this poem appeared in the Virginia City *Madisonian:*

> There came from the Rockies,
>   Far away in the West,
> A steed called Spokane
>   That of racers is best
> Of all the gay flyers
>   That ever was seen,
> For he came from Montana
>   Where the grass grows green.
> Spokane! Spokane!
>   You are a dandy flyer
> And you go from Montana
>   Where the grass grows higher.

Spokane went on to win two more big races: the American Derby at Churchill Downs and the Clark Stakes in Chicago. In both those races, he beat the mighty Proctor Knott and, altogether, won $28,000 for his owner. That was a lot of money for the time. Spokane's fame spread far and wide.

Spokane's fame spread. The people of Spokane Falls, Washington, had a fabulous blanket worth $5,000 made for Spokane. But soon after his three great victories, on July 4, 1889, Spokane lost a race to Proctor Knott, and he never won again. He retired when he was only four years old and eventually came back to Montana. The little copper-colored horse that made Montana famous lived a long life at the Doncaster Farm. He died in 1916 and is buried there.

Montana's "dandy flyer" did what no other horse has ever done. He was the only three-year-old to win all three great races. Those in the grandstands who saw the Kentucky Derby realized what a miracle they witnessed. For that brief moment in time, Spokane was a spirit horse like no other, before or since.

Just as the Great Spirit predicted, the horse named Spokane truly "accomplished the impossible," and the fiery souls of the wild Indian horses came together before a crowd of thousands. Spokane's fame lives on in the history of horse racing.

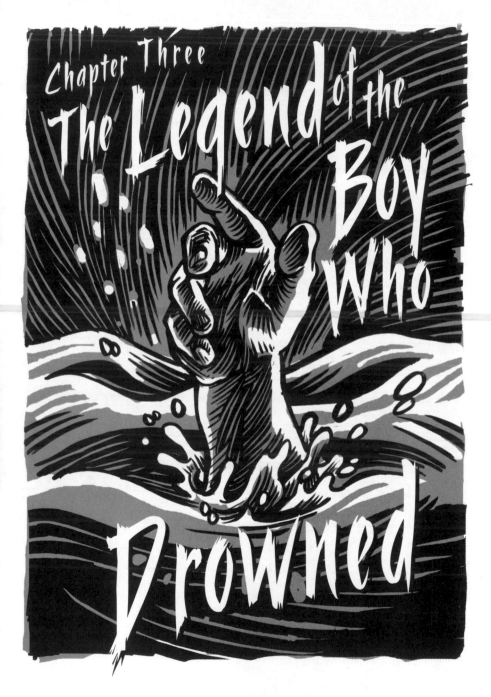

*D*OES A RESTLESS SPIRIT ROAM THE LOFTY HALLS OF THE former Great Falls Central High School? Could it be the ghost of a student from the distant past? Or is it something else?

Built back in 1896, the large, two-and-a-half-story school was constructed in an unusual way. First, sheepherders drove a herd of sheep around the site one hundred times to trample down the dirt. Then builders transported huge logs to Great Falls by floating them down the Missouri River. These logs, shaved flat on all four sides, became the beams for the floor supports, the attic framework, and the stairways. The massive blocks of sandstone that formed the walls came from a quarry near Helena. The original blackboards are still in place after more than a century.

Laughter from students long ago seems to echo through the rooms. Today the sturdy stone walls hold memories—and maybe something more.

Some of the school's former students believe that the building is haunted. According to legend, the ghost was the victim of a tragic drowning. "The Legend of the Boy who Drowned" goes back as far as 1930.

As the story goes, a boy at the school was deathly afraid of water. Historic maps of the building show that the old part of the basement once had a swimming pool, called a "plunge." It is said that a boy was standing at the edge of the plunge, which was ten feet deep all around. His friends were acting silly and pushed him in. Perhaps they did not know that the boy could not swim. The boy disappeared below the surface and did not come up. After that, school officials drained the plunge, closed it up, and locked the door. The Great Falls newspaper carried no headlines about the accident. Those who believe in the drowning think that the school district wanted to cover up the terrible accident.

The old school closed in 1975, and its halls went quiet. A few years later, it reopened as an art museum called Paris Gibson Square, named after the founder of Great Falls. It wasn't long before museum staff heard the tale about the boy who drowned. Did it really happen? If there was a drowning, what was the real story? And *is* there a ghost in Paris Gibson Square?

In 1999, reporter Carol Bradley of the *Great Falls Tribune* set out to discover, once and for all, the truth behind the legendary drowning. She did some excellent detective work. And she discovered that memories do not always preserve facts.

Carol first interviewed a former school superintendent. He said that he heard the accident happened in the 1910s. He thought that the school then drained the plunge and locked it. Museum staff at Paris Gibson Square tracked down a ninety-eight-year-old graduate from the Central High class of 1919. He remembered the story all right. He did not remember the boy's name, but he added one critical detail. He knew there had been a drowning because the victim's parents were friends of his parents. He remembered that the boy's father was a dealer of John Deere tractors. Carol went to the city directories and found that a George G. Mill had a John Deere dealership in Great Falls in 1915.

The next step was to discover if George Mill had a son who died. Carol found that George died in 1952, and from his obituary, she learned that he had a son named Grant, who died in 1915. In the 1915–1916 Central High School yearbook, Carol found a memorial page to Grant Mill. Could this be the drowning victim?

Carol was getting close. She visited Highland Cemetery and asked the caretaker to check the burial records for the Mill family. He found Grant Mill listed in the record book. Date of death: October 15, 1915. Cause of death: *accidental drowning!* Carol went back to the newspaper microfilm and looked up that date. She found the whole story buried on page twelve.

Young Grant Mill was boating with friends on the Missouri River. He did not know how to swim and was terrified of the water. That part of the story was true. Grant somehow slipped off the boat. The motor prevented his three friends from hearing the splash. When they saw him in the water flailing his arms in the air, they quickly circled back but Grant had gone under. He never surfaced again. They found his body several hours later.

There were threads of truth preserved in the story, but the facts had become muddled. When there is nothing written down, passing facts from person to person becomes very much like the game Telephone. In that game, when one person whispers a phrase and passes it on down the line through numerous players, what comes out in the end is often nothing like the original sentence. This story shows how passing down stories by word of mouth brings twists and turns to the original facts.

So is there a ghost at Paris Gibson Square? Since the old high school became an art center, children's art classes have been a popular activity. And over the last quarter of a century, art teachers have reported some chilling experiences. Several teachers in particular have reported seeing the image of a little boy.

One of these teachers had a class of first and second graders during the fall session of 2001. One day, the students had been painting. Several of the children asked to take their paintings home, but they went off and forgot them.

The class was over, and the teacher stood at the sink cleaning the paintbrushes. She heard what sounded like footsteps enter the room. Out of the corner of her eye, she saw a little boy wearing a striped shirt. He was the same height and age of the students in her class, so she assumed it was one of her aspiring little artists.

"Please wait a minute," said the teacher, "and I will help you find your painting."

The teacher turned away to put down the paintbrushes. When she looked back a few seconds later, the little boy was gone. She walked out into the hallway and looked up and down. No one was there. She asked the man working the front desk if he had seen a little boy in a striped shirt. He said that they had been alone in the building for the past forty-five minutes. He had locked the door after the last student left. The teacher shivered when she heard this, and a wave of goose bumps spread over her. She had seen the little boy just twenty minutes before.

Was this little boy a ghost? Or something else? Children work hard at what they love. They also sleep well during naptimes and at night, and they dream about their day's activities. Sometimes when people dream very hard and vividly about a place, their "essence" appears to people in the place they are dreaming about (see Sylvia Browne's story on page 9). Children dream much more vividly than adults. Maybe this little boy was dreaming about his artwork. In dreaming so hard about it, perhaps his "essence" roamed the basement hallway, looking for his forgotten painting. 🌀

IT WAS DECEMBER 30, 1924, AND FRAGRANT FLOWERS FILLED the great stone house. In the main room were the most beautiful blossoms. Beneath them: a coffin.

The peaceful face of the dead woman was even more beautiful. Mary Elling looked like an angel. Dozens of sorrowful friends filed past the open casket to pay their last respects. Although Mary has been gone now for ninety years, some say she still watches over the great stone house in Virginia City.

Mary's husband, Henry, was the wealthiest man in Madison County. Henry had come to the United States from Germany when he was only fifteen. Henry studied English, worked as a farmhand, and saved his money. In 1864, he decided to travel to the mining camp of Virginia City, Montana, where he started a business selling supplies to miners. Henry worked hard to make his fortune.

Mary Cooley moved from Vermont to Virginia City with her parents in 1865. She and Henry were married in 1870. By this time, Henry had begun to deal in gold dust. He was good at it, too. He could tell by the color exactly where the dust had come from, and he could figure its weight without a scale. Henry founded several banks and became president of others across Montana. Henry bought a corner lot on Idaho Street in Virginia City in 1876, and there he built a large and expensive home. By Virginia City standards, it was almost a mansion.

The grand, rambling stone house had gables, porches, and a white picket fence. It was a good thing the house was large because the Ellings had ten children. Three children died, but the other seven grew up in the great stone house, and Mary was a gentle mother to them all.

Mary loved to open her house for parties and special occasions. She was a good hostess and very kind to those less fortunate. Sometimes it was hard for her to be married to such a successful banker. Henry did not approve of her parties, and he did not become rich without some ruthless business dealings. And when someone could not pay his or her debts, Henry was not one to give second chances.

In 1900, Henry became sick with pneumonia and died four days later. Mary grieved for her husband. She then used the three million dollars Henry left behind to smooth over the bad feelings he had caused with some of the townsfolk. She donated money to help build Virginia City's Episcopal Church. Then she did something else. Mary built a ballroom at the back of her house.

Mary built the ballroom so that she could do what her husband had never allowed: she invited *everyone*—from her richest friends to the poorest townsfolk—to her parties. For the next twenty years, Mary gave wonderful parties, opening her home to all. There was always plenty of food, music, and dancing. The people of Virginia City loved Mary Elling. It was no wonder that the entire community grieved when she died.

Mary's children kept the house for many years, but mostly it sat empty and neglected. The sturdy stone walls Henry had built were soon covered beneath vines and weeds. The chimney collapsed. The picket fence lost all its white paint.

The house sat abandoned for a long time. Drab, sagging, and perched on a gentle slope, it looked like the perfect haunted house. The graves of both Mary and Henry sat high upon the ridge in Hillside Cemetery overlooking the town. There was a clear view of the house from the Elling family plot. If Mary's spirit were restless, she would know that her home was in a terrible state of decay.

For years, John Ellingsen was overseer of many Virginia City buildings, including the decaying Elling House. An important part of John's job was to make daily rounds, making sure vandals and thieves did no damage.

After a while, John began to notice something strange about the Elling House. When he walked past, he could see that, one by one, the windows were being broken. The odd thing was, though, that the broken glass seemed to fall on the *outside* of the

Does the ghost of Mary Elling still walk the halls of her stone house in Virginia City?
PHOTO BY ELLEN BAUMLER.

house. This meant that someone *inside* the house was breaking the windows.

John was determined to stop the vandalism. He had been in the old house several other times, and he did not like it one bit. He always felt uncomfortable, like someone was watching him. It was creepy. Yet he had to do his job, so he worked up his courage.

John figured that someone must have entered through the old ballroom door, so he collected some tools and wood so he could board it up once and for all.

The hardworking caretaker climbed the steps to the front door and slid his key into the lock. He jostled the key until the old lock released. The large, wooden door creaked as he slowly pushed it open.

John carefully made his way to the ballroom at the rear of the house. He looked around. Everything seemed to be in order. So he a took a two-by-four, knelt down, and held up the board across the doorway, intending to nail it on. He drew back his hammer, ready to pound the first nail. Then, *something grubbed his wrist*. He struggled. He could not move his arm! Whatever it was, it would not let him hit the nail.

John did not know what to do. Terrified, he put the hammer down and leaned against the far wall. When minutes passed and nothing happened, he decided it must have been his imagination. Again he held up the board to the doorway and drew back his hammer. The same thing happened again! Try as he might, John could never hit the first nail. Stunned, he grabbed his tools and left the house. He did not set foot in the Elling House again for many, many years.

John believes it was Mary Elling's ghost who grabbed his wrist that day, determined to prevent him from boarding up her beloved ballroom. She had devoted her life to welcoming the townspeople of Virginia City to her home for parties, and she simply couldn't allow someone to bar the entry. Even in death, Mary wanted to be a good hostess.

Years passed, and Toni James, a Virginia City businesswoman, purchased the Elling House. She brought the old house back to life. For the first time in decades, lights twinkled in the rooms in the evenings. Surely, Mary was pleased with this progress after so many years of neglect.

A few years ago, Toni decided to sell the great stone house. Although the sale never happened and Toni still owns the house, the couple who wanted to buy it began work on fixing up the ballroom. Starting with the wallpaper, they searched for just the right pattern. It had to look old-fashioned—a pattern that might have been in the home when it was built. There was no way to know what wallpaper Mary originally had chosen for her ballroom. The couple brought in a number of books of wallpaper samples, stacked them up on the floor of the ballroom, then left to run errands.

When they came back to the house, one of the big books was open to a page with a flowered pattern. Without giving it much thought, they closed the book. But the next day, the book was again open to the page with the flowered wallpaper pattern. That seemed a little strange. So they put the book on the bottom of the stack. Once again they returned to the room to find the same book opened to the same page.

It was time for the ballroom renovations to begin. The first task: removing the many layers of wallpaper that had accumulated over more than 100 years. As each layer peeled loose, it was interesting to see the different patterns from different time periods. Off the layers came, one at a time. Finally, the last layer came into view, the very pattern Mary Elling had chosen when her ballroom was built. The pattern on the wall was nearly identical to the pattern in the book that kept opening to the same page.

It seems that the ghost of Mary Elling was guiding the hands of those who wanted to bring her beautiful ballroom back to life.

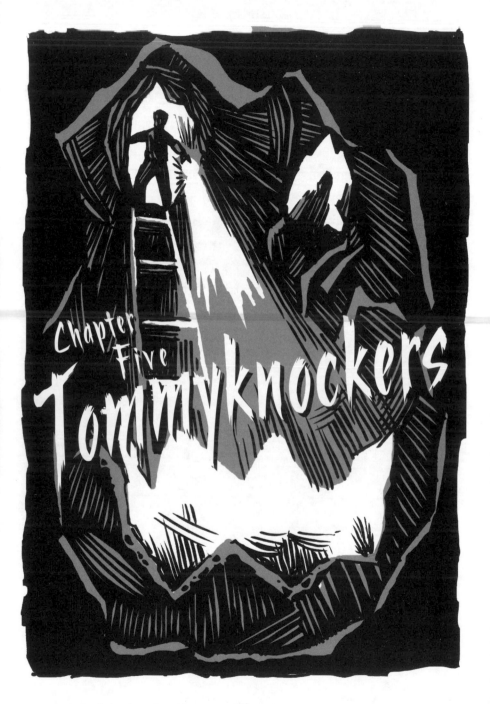

Chapter Five

Tommyknockers

Hear them knocking—listen—there!
Ghosts of miners—fighting for air.
Faint—far away—down the stope—
Picking the cave in—and no hope.
In the Leadville mines, and at Granite too—
In the Coeur d'Alenes, and the Comstock lodes,
And in the soft coal mines, where gas explodes—
Hear them! Listen—quiet—there!
Ghosts of miners—wanting air.

— FROM "GHOSTS," BY JOHN C. FROHLICHER

Tap. Tap. Tap. As miners long ago worked in the dark, wet mining shafts in southwestern Montana, they heard strange, disturbing sounds. Some men believed that the ghosts of dead miners, buried alive beneath tons of rock during cave-ins, were *tap, tap, tapping* away for eternity. Others said the sounds came from something more sinister.

Today, there are many old abandoned mines in the mountains and hills of southwestern Montana. It is important to be *very* careful of these abandoned mines—and not just because of ghosts. Scattered mining holes and piles of dirt from the diggings (called "tailings") are dangerous and best left alone. Miners who worked the hills for gold, silver, copper, and coal could tell you just how dangerous they are. They would also tell you that sometimes miners left more than tunnels and piles of tailings. They sometimes left their souls. Tom Donovan and his buddies made this discovery late one night many years ago.

Tom grew up in Missoula. He loved to hunt in the hills of southwestern Montana with his friends. When Tom was in high school, he had a scary experience that he never forgot. And to this day, he cannot explain it.

It was a Friday afternoon, and the weekend lay ahead. He and three friends decided it would be a good weekend for a hunting trip. They packed their sleeping bags, their flashlights, their guns, and some food and piled into the car. It was almost dark when they finally left town. Soon the lights of Missoula were behind them.

The boys drove into the hills where they had hunted many times before. This area in the Garnet Range was known for its

veins of gold running deep underground. Miners from England, Ireland, Germany, and many other places came to the area seeking their fortunes. Most miners were superstitious because working underground was so dangerous and because strange things happened beneath the earth.

For example, just before a mine collapses, the timbers deep in the tunnels begin to creak. Then comes an eerie, hollow knocking. This knocking foretells the coming cave-in, when it is too late to escape. The very thought of the hollow *"knock, knock, knock"* was enough to send shivers down the spines of even the most courageous miners.

Imagine what it would be like. Deep underground, the darkness surrounds you. If your light goes out, you are helpless. Finding your way without a candle or a flashlight is impossible. The small tunnels were supported only by log beams, which were not always strong enough to hold back the tons of earth above. Cave-ins were common. A miner could die at any moment. And collapses were not the only danger. Stale air could quickly suffocate you. There were also explosions, fires, floods, equipment failures, and human errors. Any of these could cost a man his life. Living with that knowledge was a fearsome thing.

Tom and his buddies, though, gave little thought to mining disasters as they drove into the foothills of the Garnet Range. Their minds were on the hunting trip. As they drove along the lonely dirt road, they realized that this was a very dark night indeed. The boys decided that they had better find a place to stop and make camp. They wanted to get plenty of sleep so they could get an early start in the morning.

The teens found a spot along the dirt road that looked like a good place to camp. They pulled over, grabbed their sleeping bags, and hiked a short distance from the road. The boys made a fire and had a bite to eat. It was so dark that they couldn't tell how far up the road they had traveled. They decided to figure that out the next morning, when it was light.

Each boy found a spot for his sleeping bag. The ground seemed to have some soft depressions, but it was free of stones and bumps. *What a great campsite,* Tom thought as he rolled out his sleeping bag amid the glow of the fire. After a little bit of talk around the campfire, the boys settled into the warmth of their sleeping bags. Each boy quickly fell asleep.

It was close to midnight. All four boys suddenly awoke at the same time. *Tap. Tap. Tap.* They sat up in their sleeping bags. *Tap. Tap. Tap.*

The fire was out, and the boys couldn't see one another. Startled out of sleep, they whispered, "What is that? Do you hear that noise?"

Tap. Tap. Tap. The sound seemed muffled and slightly distant, like it was coming from somewhere underground. It was steady and regular, almost like the beat in a song. *Tap. Tap. Tap.*

What the boys did not know is that the miners who prospected these hills long ago heard noises in the mines—and said they knew where the sounds came from. These Cornish miners, from Cornwall, England, said "little men" lived underground and caused the knocking with their tiny hammers just before a cave-in. The Cornish called them "tommyknockers."

Some miners believed that the tommyknockers were good

spirits who warned miners just before the mine collapsed—but that the first miner to hear their knocking was doomed to die. Others believed that the tommyknockers actually caused the disaster with their hammering. Good tommyknockers were believed to bring wealth to those they favored. The evil ones brought bad luck. They played mischievous tricks like stealing tools or lunch buckets. And they liked to hurt miners who did not believe in them.

As the decades passed, some miners began to believe that the tommyknockers were the spirits of dead miners. The tommyknockers swung their picks. *Tap. Tap. Tap.* They shoveled rock, working side by side with the living miners. *Tap. Tap. Tap.* They warned of disaster. Miners even left offerings for them at the entrances to mines. They hoped that food and drink would keep the tommyknockers happy and bring good luck.

Belief in the tommyknockers was so strong that some miners refused to work where others had experienced bad luck. Sometimes miners even abandoned these unlucky mines, fearing that the bad luck was the work of tommyknockers.

Tap. Tap. Tap. Tom and his friends grabbed their flashlights and turned them into the darkness, panning the forest for the source of the sound. They huddled together, trying to figure out what it was. The sound was very distinct. Like a pick hitting rock. And it seemed to be coming from directly beneath them.

Trying to calm themselves, they decided that some miner must be working—but why would someone be up here mining at midnight?

Tom and his three friends crawled out of their warm sleeping bags, shivering in the cold night air. They took their flashlights and followed the eerie sound. Mineshafts, holes in the earth dropping straight down, could be anywhere. The boys knew to be careful. A fall down one of these deep holes could be fatal. They knew they should not be wandering in the dark. But there was something about the sound that drew them toward it. They could not help themselves.

They seemed to be getting closer. *Tap. Tap. Tap.* Tom swung his flashlight to the left, and it shone upon a large hole just a few feet away. As they slowly approached, they realized the sound was getting louder.

As the four boys looked down the gaping mouth of the mineshaft, they saw an old wooden ladder. They knew it was dangerous, but the mystery was irresistible. Then the boys did what no one should ever do: they began to climb down the ladder.

Tap. Tap. Tap. The forest was dark, but the darkness in the shaft was even blacker, and the echo of the sound grew louder as the boys made their way down the ladder, one by one. *TAP. TAP. TAP.* As they struggled to find their footing in the dark, they aimed their flashlights along the walls of the shaft and could see that they were wet and slimy. Water trickled down the sides. They could hear it. *Drip. Drip. Drip.*

There was a pool of water at the bottom, and as the first boy down the ladder stepped into it, the sound of the pick suddenly stopped, cut off in mid-tap. Tunnels ran in all directions, and the boys had no idea which way to go. The quiet was even worse than the mysterious tapping sound. All they could hear was the *drip, drip, drip* of the slimy water.

Terrified, they scrambled back up the ladder, climbed out of the hole, and raced through the dense trees back to their campsite. Feeling safe, they started the fire again and made some hot chocolate. After a few minutes of silence, they began to talk about what had just happened. They couldn't explain it. Who was mining deep in the earth at midnight? Maybe they didn't want to know.

The forest was quiet. The sounds were gone. So the boys decided that they would remain huddled together by the fire until morning. They crawled back into their sleeping bags. None of them slept.

When the first streaks of dawn appeared in the sky, the boys got up. They packed up their gear, put out their fire, and made their way back to the car. They could see in the early light that there was a sign by the road. They had made camp near the ghost town of Coloma. They could now see the outlines of empty, crumbling cabins and small buildings.

By the thin light of early dawn, the boys went back to check their camp and make sure they had not left anything behind. As they hiked the short distance from the road to their campsite, they made a horrifying discovery. Their camp was in the middle of the mining camp's cemetery.

The boys stood over the blackened remains of their campfire. There were no tombstones, but they could see where the graves were. The earth had settled, leaving soft depressions. They had spent the night on top of Coloma's dead.

Today, Tom has no explanation for the eerie sounds he and his buddies heard that night long ago. But he and his friends are not alone in finding Coloma a mysterious place. Archaeologists

from the University of Montana have recently been studying the area to learn more about its history. According to the Bureau of Land Management, there is very little information about the town. Some believe people moved away because the mines were failures. Others think there are still fortunes awaiting discovery in the hills around Coloma.

Could the *tap, tap, tap* of the miner's pick deep underground be the work of tommyknockers? Deep in the underground they swing their picks, these spirits of dead miners who mine there no more. *Tap. Tap. Tap.*

And we leave the haunted place,
For we won't work where 'ere they be,
And wherever we hear them knockin'
We sure will always flee.
For it means whoever hears it
Will be the next in line,
For the pick-pick of the Tommy Knockers
Is the last and awful sign.

— ADAPTED FROM "TOMMY KNOCKERS," BY ANTHONY FITCH

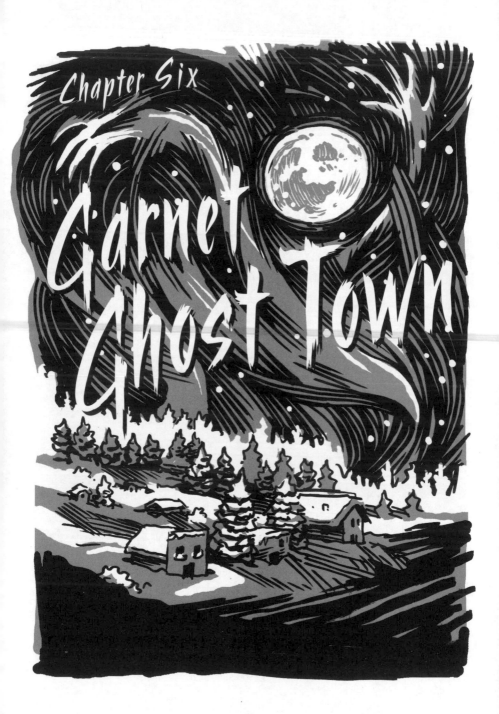

Chapter Six

Garnet Ghost Town

MIDNIGHT IS THE "WITCHING HOUR"—A TIME WHEN supernatural creatures are said to emerge from their shadowy world into ours. They say that when the witching hour creeps upon the clock at Garnet, ghostly fingers strike ivory keys. Piano music floats across the empty buildings as the spirits of Garnet play their ghostly music and dance their ghostly dance.

Six thousand feet up a mountainside between Helena and Missoula lies the ghost town of Garnet. This eerie collection of tumbledown buildings was once a busy town full of people.

Garnet's first (living) citizens named their town after the pretty, dark-red stones they found there. But people came to Garnet for the gold. In the late 1800s, more than 1,000 people lived in Garnet. There were thirteen saloons, four stores, four busy hotels, and a school with forty-one students. A stagecoach took travelers down the mountain to the towns of Bearmouth and Drummond and back again every day. Miners crowded into the boardinghouses, where they ate their meals and slept soundly. They worked long shifts at the twenty mines in the area. Garnet was full of life at all times of the day and night. And even when the clock struck midnight, the piano player's music in Kelley's Saloon didn't end. The music drifted out the doorway, tinkling in the night.

By 1905, much of the gold was gone, and the first residents moved on. Only about 150 people still lived in Garnet. Then, in 1912, a terrible fire began at the Garnet Hotel and burned half the buildings in town. Many owners did not want to build again, so they left. Only a few stayed.

In 1923, when only a handful of people still lived in Garnet, Elizabeth Farmer Smith was ten years old. Her father, Charles Farmer, worked at the mines. Elizabeth spent her summers there. The Fourth of July was the best time of all. The whole town turned out to dance in the great hall with the wooden floor, dancing all night as the piano player's skilled fingers raced across the ivory keys.

As much as Elizabeth loved summers at Garnet, there was one person she and the other children feared. That was a stern-looking man named Frank Davey, who owned just about everything in town. He owned the stagecoach line and the one hotel left over from the old days. He also owned the town's only general store and most of the land around Garnet. Elizabeth could spend hours looking at all the things for sale in Mr. Davey's store. Nails, old-fashioned shoes, and tools were in the front, groceries were in the middle, and the meat shop was at the back. He had an icehouse, where he kept the meat and other items that would spoil. Inside the icehouse, built into the back wall, were three secret compartments. There, Mr. Davey stored the gold that came from the mines, and he guarded it with great care.

Even though Elizabeth and the other children loved the general store, they were afraid of Mr. Davey. He was not a friendly man, and he always spoke gruffly to his young customers. Mr. Davey's hair was white, and he dressed in a stodgy, three-piece suit. He glared at the children when they came into the store, and he watched their every move. Old Mr. Davey didn't trust the children not to sneak a piece of the penny candy he kept behind the counter. He guarded the counter like he guarded the gold.

The older boys sometimes played mean tricks on Mr. Davey. First, they would ask to buy some candy. Then, when Mr. Davey put the sacks of treats on the counter, the boys put rocks on the counter instead of money, grabbed the sacks, and ran away. Mr. Davey pretended to be very angry, and he threatened to tell their parents. It was a kind of mean game he played. Secretly, though, he told his friends that he thought it was funny that the little children were afraid of him and that the older ones thought he was so mean. As long as there were children in Garnet, Mr. Davey played his little games.

The children of Garnet did not like Mr. Davey or his games one bit. One day, they found some old clothes like the ones

Garnet ghost town sleeps under a blanket of snow. Ghosts are particularly active in Garnet during winter, and visitors spot transparent figures in old-fashioned clothes walking the streets. Ghostly footprints in the snow are sometimes seen entering buildings but not coming back out. PHOTO BY ALLAN MATHEWS.

he wore and stuffed them with straw. Then they hanged "Mr. Davey" from the flagpole.

Years passed, and Elizabeth grew up. Most people moved away from Garnet, but Frank Davey stayed. He lived all alone in the spooky, three-story hotel he owned. But the hotel had no more guests, and there were no more children to scare. There was only old Mr. Davey and the ghosts of the past.

Mr. Davey died in 1947. By then, no one was left in Garnet. However, the creepy old hotel, Mr. Davey's store, Kelley's

Saloon, some of the old cabins, and other buildings are still there today, abandoned.

Or are they?

To this day, tourists sometimes claim to hear the faint sound of the piano drifting through the empty saloon. And people who visit Garnet in winter—most especially during the witching hour—see things. Startling things.

In the cold winter months, snow falls softly on the ghost town. The weathered boards and rooftops peek out from white blankets. Late at night, the spirits of Garnet come out to play in the moonlight. Sometimes, in the deep winter quiet, a piano tinkles in Kelley's Saloon and the spirits dance to the ghostly music. Men's voices echo in the empty rooms. But the moment a living, human hand touches the building, the noises stop.

Winter visitors who come by snowmobile tell of transparent figures walking the streets and wearing the fashions of long ago. Doors open and close inside the hollow buildings, and footsteps trudge up the stairway in the old hotel. Footprints in freshly fallen snow lead into the buildings, but the footprints never come out.

Garnet's ghosts especially like to play when the snow piles high and the mountain air is thin and cold. They cause no trouble, and anyone who visits the deserted town in the dead of winter should be prepared to meet them. They hide in the shadows, laugh in the wind, and come out when you least expect them.

The ghosts sometimes reveal themselves in the summer, too. Park ranger Allan Mathews, who works for the Bureau of Land Management, knows this all too well. According to Ranger Mathews, on a recent summer day a volunteer was working at the visitor center. Three tourists—a woman and her two kids—came in and asked, "Who's that man over there, standing at the door of the icehouse, with his arms spread out funny?"

The volunteer looked in the direction of the icehouse, where old Mr. Davey stored his gold. She did not see anyone. The confused volunteer asked the family to describe him. One of the kids said, "He has white hair, and he's wearing a three-piece suit, and he looks really mean."

Their mother nodded in agreement.

The volunteer shrugged and said that it was probably just another visitor. She did not want to scare them. She did not tell them what she knew. The volunteer realized that, after all this time, old Mr. Davey's ghost still stands guard over his gold shipments—and that he likes to scare kids, to get back at them for all their mean tricks.

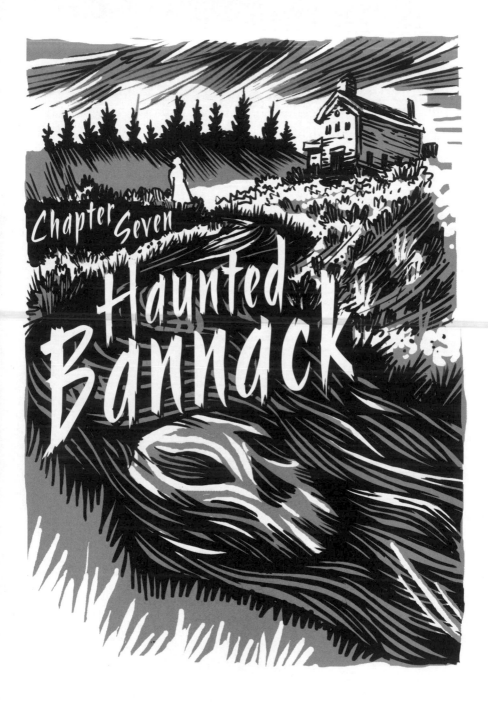

Chapter Seven

Haunted Bannack

THE HISTORY OF THE TOWN OF BANNACK IS FULL OF tragedy. There were hangings, shootouts, and illnesses. Many of Bannack's dead lie buried on the hillside in the town's lonely cemetery. And not all of them rest in peace. Visitors sometimes catch glimpses of spirits playing hide-and-seek in the empty buildings. Sometimes you can hear their lonely cries as the wind carries their voices into the surrounding hills.

Gold discovered on nearby Grasshopper Creek in 1862 brought miners across the mountains and over the Continental Divide. They were hungry for golden treasure. The town of Bannack quickly sprouted up, becoming the capital of Montana Territory in 1864.

The Meade Hotel is one of Bannack's most haunted places. There are good reasons. The large brick hotel once served as the courthouse, where dramatic and highly emotional trials took place. And in 1877, the brick structure was the best place to hide when rumors circulated that Chief Joseph and a band of Nez Perce Indians were coming to attack Bannack. Terrified men, women, and children blocked the doors with furniture and huddled inside for a whole week. Although the Nez Perce never came, surely the terrible fear of attack left an impression in the old building.

Then in 1888, Dr. John S. Meade and his wife, Louisa, moved to Bannack with their large family. The Meades bought the old courthouse and remodeled it as the Meade Hotel. The courtroom and county headquarters became a lobby, parlors, and dining hall, and the offices upstairs became bedrooms. Louisa set the tables with white linen, and guests enjoyed delicious meals prepared in the kitchen at the back.

The Meade children grew up in Bannack. They played in the hotel and explored the mine tailings left near the banks of Grasshopper Creek.

When children in Bannack were sick, the home of miner Amede Bessett and his wife became a hospital. The Bessetts had a large two-story house. The upstairs was one long room where sick children could be isolated and cared for. Diseases like measles spread quickly. It was important to separate sick children so that others did not catch the disease. Before the use of vaccines, children often died from common childhood diseases. Dr. Meade and Louisa, a trained army nurse who served in the Civil War, used their medical training to tend to the children. When the

Meades' grandson became ill, they did everything they could for him, but the little boy died. Life in Bannack was sometimes cruel.

Today, the Bessett House is known as the "house of crying babies." Most visitors do not know about the children who died of measles in the Bessett House. These visitors sometimes remark that when they visit the upstairs, they hear the faint sound of babies crying. It is very disturbing.

After their grandson's death, the Meades had had enough of Montana. They packed their belongings and moved to California, leaving the hotel to others.

The years went by, and Bannack had many terrible tragedies for a town so small. Three-year-old Velma Thompson drowned in Grasshopper Creek in 1909. In 1911, two little children died when their house burned down.

After the Meades left, Rufus Mathews and his wife, Montie, took over running the Meade Hotel. The Mathews had four children. Their youngest child, Bertie, spent much of her childhood roaming the halls of the converted courthouse. She was only ten when her father died, and she and her sisters helped their mother with the hotel.

When Bertie was fifteen, the Dunn family moved to Bannack. The Dunns had a daughter, Dorothy, who was exactly Bertie's age. There were few children in Bannack, and Bertie was thrilled to have someone her own age in town. Dorothy and Bertie became best friends.

On a hot August afternoon in 1916, Dorothy, her sister Fern, and their friend Ruth Wornick waded into Grasshopper Creek just down the way from town. The water felt cool and inviting.

Forgetting the danger, the girls waded out from the bank into a place where the water made a little pool. Twenty years before, dredge boats moved up and down the creek. They had worked this area, taking big bites out of the creek bottom to get the gold buried there.

Dorothy, Fern, and Ruth all knew the dredging had left the creek bed uneven, but they were so hot and the water felt so good that before they knew it they had waded too far out. Suddenly, the ground disappeared beneath their feet. They stepped off a shelf into water nine feet deep, carved out by the dredge. None of the girls could swim. Twelve-year-old Smith Paddock heard their screams and ran to help. He pulled Ruth and Fern out of the water, but Dorothy went under and never came up. The hole made by the dredge where the creek bed gives way to deep water is known to this day as "Dorothy's Hole."

Bertie took the loss of her friend very hard. Sometime after Dorothy's death, Bertie was upstairs in the hotel, making beds. She looked up from her work to see the ghost of her dead friend. She instantly knew who it was because Bertie recognized the long blue dress Dorothy wore. Bertie lived to be ninety-one, and she remembered this experience as if it were yesterday. But it was one subject gentle Bertie did not want to talk about.

Over the years, others have had eerie experiences in the old hotel. The building has a special kind of energy. Sometimes you can feel it. Walk through the rooms, and you can feel the cold spots even on the hottest days.

Children often have strange experiences in the Meade Hotel. The Bryson family's seven-year-old daughter Abbey had one of these encounters in June 1997. Abbey and her dad were in one of the upstairs hotel rooms. Her dad turned to go and got halfway down the stairs when he realized Abbey wasn't behind him. So he went back to the room to get her. He saw her standing in the dark, staring. There was nothing there, but Abbey's attention seemed fixed on something her dad could not see. He almost had to carry her out of the room. Later, Abbey explained that Dorothy was in the dark room with her. It seemed as if she had something to say. Abbey tried hard to hear what Dorothy wanted to tell her. Even though Dorothy's mouth was moving, Abbey said that there was no sound coming out.

Sometimes visitors to Bannack find themselves short of breath. On the evening of June 27, 2003, tour guide Michael Staley experienced this firsthand. He was giving a tour of the old hotel to some Boy Scouts when one of them became separated from the group. Michael got everyone out and went back in to search. He climbed the stairs. As he reached the top step, he felt the air grow thin and noticed that he was out of breath. It was as if there was not enough oxygen for him to breathe. He made his way down the hallway, breathing hard. He saw the boy, glassy eyed and ghastly white, standing in a doorway to one of the hotel rooms. The boy seemed frozen there, unable to move. Michael pulled him toward the stairs. They tumbled down the grand spiral staircase and stumbled out the door, both of them gasping for air. They said it was like being underwater, drowning, and unable to breathe. Were they experiencing what poor Dorothy Dunn had when she drowned in Grasshopper Creek?

In the late spring of 2005, a group of adult students gathered at Bannack. They spent the day wandering around the town and exploring the cemetery. The summer sun was very hot that day. Throughout the afternoon, one student and then another entered the Meade Hotel to escape the heat. Everyone agreed the building was unusually cool, and in some places there were definite cold spots. Standing in these areas brought a shiver down the spine.

Night began to fall, and the other tourists left the park. Darkness began to fill the shadows and creep into the doorways of the empty buildings. The park staff and the students gathered in the front room of the Meade Hotel to discuss the day's activities.

 There were perhaps twenty people in the front room of the old hotel, and because there were no chairs or furniture, the students sat on the stairs. They filled the graceful curving stairwell halfway up to the second story. Park superintendent Tom Lowe and

several staff leaned against the wall in the lobby. One by one, the students shared their experiences and feelings about Bannack. Group leader Patrick Marsolek, of Helena, had been careful to make sure the students did not know much of the history of the Meade Hotel or its haunted tales. Each person took a turn sharing his or her feelings. Almost everyone mentioned the odd, clammy, cold spots in certain rooms of the Meade Hotel. None of the students, however, knew about Dorothy Dunn.

An hour later, the Meade was in total darkness. Eyes adjusted to the pitch black, and you could barely make out the shapes of the people sitting on the stairway. Only one student, Kim Newman, had not spoken. Kim got up from her seat near the bottom of the stairs and stood in the middle of the room. She told about a dream she had:

I don't know what this means, but a few nights ago I had a vivid dream about our trip to Bannack. I dreamed that I was standing in the middle of this room in the Meade Hotel, just as I am now. I knew it was the Meade, and I was barefoot. I could feel the wood floor beneath my feet. I looked up and everything was blurry, like I was underwater, at the bottom of a pool. Then, I dreamed that I opened my mouth to speak, and water gushed out all over the floor. It was the strangest thing.

When Kim finished sharing her dream, she seemed out of breath. She took her seat on the stairs. Tom, the park superintendent, took over and stepped into the center of the room. He turned on a flashlight and began to tell the story of Dorothy Dunn.

Everyone in the room that night agreed that something strange happened. Tom told the story of Dorothy's drowning. Then he told about the apparition Bertie saw upstairs in the hotel. The upstairs was in complete darkness, but you could just make out the top of the stairway.

Suddenly, from somewhere deep in the rooms upstairs, there was a sound. Maybe it was just the old building settling. Whatever it was, everyone heard it. And the energy was so thick you could cut it with a knife.

It was very dark when the group got up to leave. As Kathy Martinka left the old hotel with the crowd, she turned and snapped a quick photo in the deep moonlight. The photograph is full of orbs—floating, circular objects that some believe reveal supernatural activity.

The Meade Hotel has another curious secret. There is a steel vault in what was once the office of the county treasurer. This vault is like a large walk-in closet. In the building's lifetime as a courthouse, the vault was a place where county officials stored records and courtroom evidence that needed locking up. The county treasurer's wife and children hid in the vault during the Nez Perce scare. The door is very heavy, and when it is shut, inside the vault there is no light at all, except for one tiny pin-prick. A peephole in the center of the door lets in a tiny amount of light. But when the light is just right, it catches one of the large front windows and acts like a projector. If you stand inside the vault with the door closed, the reflection of the window appears, life-size, on the wall inside the vault. Because of this odd and ghostly shadow, they call it "Dorothy's Window."

The tragedies at Bannack seem to forever remain a part of the town. Painful memories drift through the empty buildings, peek around the corners in the old hotel, and cry out. Pick a quiet afternoon, and see for yourself.

This photo of the Meade Hotel in Bannack shows strange floating spheres, called orbs. Many believe orbs are spirits. PHOTO BY KATHY MARTINKA.

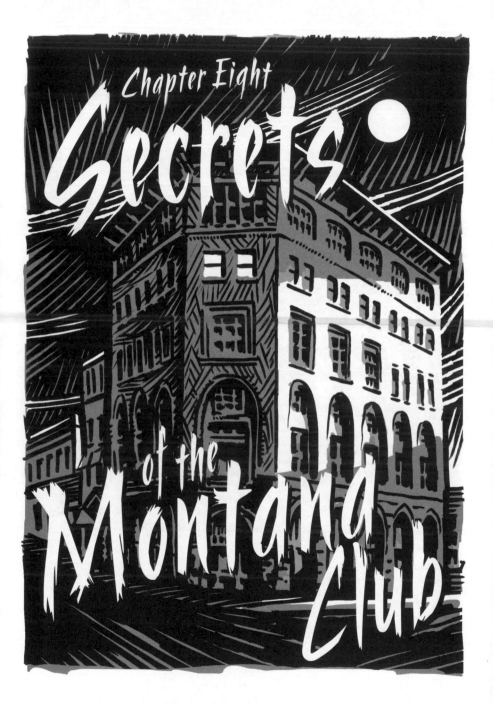

Chapter Eight

Secrets of the Montana Club

THE ELEGANT MONTANA CLUB IN HELENA HOLDS MANY secrets. Figures appear in its numerous rooms, wide hallways, and dark basement. Beneath the large, castle-like building are winding passages—and ghosts who like to play tricks.

It was here that, long ago, prominent and wealthy men planned the future of the new state of Montana. Members organized the men-only club in 1885 to bring refinement to the Montana frontier. Clubs for men only were common in the nineteenth century. Members built the first club building in 1893 and many of them lived in the club's rented rooms. The club had a game room, a dining room, a reading room, and a billiards room. There was even a bowling alley in the basement.

The club had one of the first elevators in Helena. These early elevators needed someone to run them. In 1903, the club hired fourteen-year-old Harry Anderson to take members up and down the floors of the fancy six-story building. Harry was the son of the club's bartender, Julian Anderson. Harry had a secret that not even his father knew. Harry liked to start fires.

He wanted to start a little fire, one that the firemen could easily put out. Young, reckless Harry took the elevator to the sixth floor. He checked the hall. It was late in the evening, and all was quiet. Harry had been waiting for just this moment. He lit a match and dropped it on a burlap flour sack. The impulsive young elevator operator watched as the flames licked at the edges of the sack. Then it burst into flames. Foolishly, Harry thought, *It's just a small fire.*

Harry scurried down the hallway and took the elevator to the first floor. The fire quickly began to spread. Toy, the club's Chinese cook, discovered the flames. Soon Harry heard the clanging of the fire alarm. He ran to help as the horse-drawn teams clattered to a stop, with the town's fire wagon in tow. Harry helped the firemen by holding the horses while the men unrolled the hose. Wind whipped through the gulch. The April night was cold, and blowing snow swirled in the wind.

Flames crept down the six floors of the famous Montana Club. The fire department did not have ladders tall enough to reach the top floor. The water pressure in the hoses was not strong enough to reach that far, either. Harry Anderson's little fire grew into a monster. The monster ate the entire building, floor by floor. By dawn, nothing was left of the famous Montana Club except a few stone arches.

Officials investigated the fire. They discovered not only that Harry had set that fire but that he had also started other fires around town. Foolish and irresponsible Harry started the fires because he liked to hear the fire alarm ring and watch the horses come running. Then he liked to help the firemen hold the horses while the men put out the fires.

Harry was lucky the judge did not send him to the state prison at Deer Lodge. Instead, Harry went to Pine Hills, the boys' reform school at Miles City, where he spent the rest of his youth.

The ashes from the fire had hardly cooled before club members began to plan a new building. Using the same basement and reconstructing the stone arches, the new building grew out of the ashes of the old. Inside it was much like the old club.

Today, the Montana Club is much different. Both men and women can join. Much of the building is now offices. The basement's bowling alley is gone, replaced by a pub.

But impressions of the past remain. If you stand on the first floor at the bottom of the grand stairway and look up, you can see all the way to the sixth floor. Just imagine how many people traveled up and down those stairs, and up and down the elevators, in the past 100 years. Perhaps some of them never left. Could they be responsible for the strange occurrences that happen there?

J. Anne Roberts experienced one odd event a few years ago when she was the club manager. On this Saturday night, J. Anne and two employees were working late. They were cleaning up the sixth-floor dining room after a wedding reception. It was after midnight. Suddenly the phone rang, startling the three of them. J. Anne picked up the receiver.

"Hello?" she said.

"This is the Helena Police," said the caller. "Is everything all right over there?"

"Well, yes. I think so. What do you mean?" asked J. Anne.

"We've received several 911 calls," said the officer, "and the telephone identification shows that they came from inside the Montana Club."

J. Anne could not believe it. No one else was in the building, and they had not been near the telephone. Officers came and searched all the floors. They found nothing. They left shaking their heads.

"We didn't find anything," they told her. "But the building is so large and there are so many rooms that we can't guarantee the building is empty. Someone could be living here and no one would know." Police never found the mysterious caller.

Perhaps it was Harry, still wanting to hear those sirens, after all these years.

Helena businessman Al Swanson had a strange encounter at the club one day. At the top of the stairs, on the second floor, is a large reception hall. To the right of the reception hall is a tiny private dining room. The room has an unusual oval shape. When its heavy door is open, those passing through the reception hall can clearly see into this little private space.

On this particular day, Al came up the steps into the reception hall and passed by the small dining room. Out of the corner of his eye, he saw something unusual. He paused a moment to glance

into the room. He saw an elderly man hunched over a plate, eating his dinner. The man seemed sad, sitting there all by himself. Only later did Al stop to think about why an elderly man would be sitting in the private dining room all by himself. When he passed by the room again a short time later, the man was still there.

Al was curious and felt bad for the elderly gentleman sitting all alone. So he walked up to one of the servers and asked about the man in the private dining room. She looked at him blankly and said she had no idea what he was talking about. There was no one in there. He walked over to the doorway and again looked into the small room. Sure enough, there was no one there.

At the end of the day, when workers inside the Montana Club have gone home, the quiet is disturbing. Club employees who work in the dining rooms and kitchen are aware of the building's quirks. They especially do not like to go down to the basement after dark. There is a creepy feeling down there, they say. It feels like someone is always watching you.

The basement's boiler room, reminiscent of the boiler room in the haunted hotel in Stephen King's *The Shining,* is at the end of a tangled series of corridors. In this room a few years ago, in the sandy soil between where the wall and the floor join, a little gift from the past surfaced. A red cat's-eye marble caught the light, gleaming. Why was it there? To whom did it belong? Could it be Harry playing a ghostly game? No one knows.

One weekend the club hosted a private party, and the staff worked especially late. When they had finished cleaning up, they carefully locked the building. The next Monday morning, when Nord Johnson, the club manager, arrived at work, he found something weird. The elevator was stuck between floors. It had been running just fine over the weekend. He checked it over but could find nothing wrong, except that the car would not move.

Nord called the elevator technician, who came to check out the problem. The technician could find nothing wrong with the system, so he went down to the basement, and then to the dark sub-basement beneath. There he found the elevator's gearbox. The gearbox sits in an enclosed spot in the wall. It is important for the gearbox to stay free of dust. Particles of dust and dirt that get into the gears can cause damage and prevent the elevator from running smoothly.

A heavy, airtight dust plate covered the box. So the repairman got his screwdriver and carefully removed the screws, one by one. He removed the heavy plate, exposing the box for the first time in a long while. Inside he found the trouble all right, and it was unbelievable! Stuck in a gear, holding up the elevator, was a small, clear glass marble. Where the marble came from and how it got into the gearbox is a mystery.

We know that the young elevator operator Harry Anderson liked to call in alarms. Perhaps—like most boys his age—he also liked to play with marbles. Maybe Harry still likes playing tricks. All we can say for sure is that the Montana Club holds on tightly to its secrets. 🌿

Chapter
Nine The
Conrad
Mansion

How would you like to go to a Halloween ball in a fire-scorched mansion? On Halloween in 1910 in Kalispell, 500 guests attended the strangest party Montana has ever seen. Alicia Conrad, or "Lettie," as her friends called her, took great pleasure in throwing fancy parties and welcoming guests to her home. Her love for the mansion might explain why her presence lingers there today. And her warm hospitality might further explain why some claim to have seen ghostly faces of phantom guests in the windows of Kalispell's Conrad Mansion.

Lettie first came to Fort Benton, Montana, from Nova Scotia in 1879. She was highly educated, a skilled pianist, and a very proper lady. There were very few young, single women in Fort

Benton, and Lettie was very beautiful. Young men often came calling, but it was Charles E. Conrad who won her heart. They were married in 1881.

Charles helped to found the town of Kalispell, opened a bank, and moved his family there. In 1895, Charles built a mansion on a beautiful hill overlooking the valley.

Lettie Conrad welcomed everyone into her home in Kalispell and loved to throw parties. Long after Lettie's death during restoration of the mansion, a worker saw Lettie's ghostly form walking the halls.
PHOTO COURTESY OF THE MONTANA STATE HISTORIC PRESERVATION OFFICE.

Lettie loved to have company in her home. At Christmastime, she invited anyone who was alone for the holidays to come and stay at the mansion. There were guests in every nook and cranny, all over the house. The mansion's long dining room table could comfortably seat forty-five guests! Generous Lettie always opened her home on Christmas Day to needy families and gave everyone food and gifts. She was a selfless person who gave much of her time to the Salvation Army and other charities. The town of Kalispell loved her, and they loved her parties.

Charles and Lettie had three children: Charles Jr., Kate, and Alicia. When her husband died in 1902, Lettie carried on, taking care of the children and managing Charles' estate and business interests. Alicia, the youngest of the Conrads' children, and Lettie were together all the time. The years went by.

When Alicia was eighteen, she and Lettie came home from a dinner party one night in mid-October. The Halloween ball they were planning was several weeks away. They stayed up late to work on the details. Lettie finally went up to bed, and Alicia began to turn out the lights. Suddenly, she heard someone beating on the front door.

Alicia threw the door open and a man yelled, "Your house is on fire!" He pointed to the flames leaping out of the north side of the house.

While Lettie called the fire department, Alicia fought the fire. Although her mother did not know it at the time, all her life Alicia had loved to explore the roof. She would sneak out in her stocking feet, walk along the uneven ridges, and thrill to the views of the valley below. So she was quite skilled at climbing and balancing way up on top of the house. Alicia grabbed the hose and raced to the roof. There she fought the flames for what seemed like a very long time.

Finally, Alicia saw the horse-drawn fire wagon. Half the town followed behind, racing to the scene. The firemen and volunteers were able to get the flames under control. Alicia's efforts helped save the house, but water was everywhere. The volunteers from town began to use blankets to sop up the water. They formed a human chain, passing heavy, wet blankets down the line. Waiting hands wrung them out—then back they would come to sop up more.

The house suffered mostly from water damage, but the furniture, piled out of harm's way, was safe. At the end of the long night, Lettie was exhausted. She looked around her at the damage. Then she had an idea.

"Every year at Halloween time," she told Alicia, "I would just love to get on a broom and get rid of all the mischief that collects all year. You and I have always loved Halloween, probably because there is a good bit of the devil in both of us! This year we shall give the greatest Halloween party that ever was!"

Lettie and Alicia began to plan. They wanted to thank the many volunteers who had helped save the mansion, so they invited everyone who wanted to come. Lettie intended the party to be wonderful. She also wanted it to be a lesson in how to deal with misfortune. She instructed that nothing be cleaned up. The soggy fallen plaster, the piled furniture, and the gaping hole in the roof became props for a spectacular Halloween party.

And perfect it was! The fire damage helped transform the

basement and main floor into Dante's Inferno. Dante, an Italian poet, wrote frightening descriptions of hell. This became the party's theme. Guests entered "hell" by way of a circular stairway built in the elevator shaft. A guide took the guests down into the dark basement. Clammy wet canvas hung over the doorways. Workers wired beaded curtains with electricity. Passing through the curtains gave the guests a mild electric shock. All along the way, strings hung down along the dark path like cobwebs. The guide led the guests out through the coal chute, where carpenters had built another set of stairs. These led from the basement to the outside.

Outside, the guests made their way to the front door. When they stepped inside, they saw Spanish moss draped everywhere, especially over the balcony and on the chandeliers. Lettie's brother was a taxidermist. He helped out, making dozens of lifelike bats out of cardboard and silk stuffed with cotton. The bats were hung on invisible silk thread, and fans kept them flying.

The guide again led the guests to the elevator shaft. They climbed up the stairway, this time to the second-story bedrooms. There, a mass of wet, slick plaster covered the floors. The path was difficult and uneven. This was "purgatory," Dante's halfway place between hell and paradise. Gray, wet plaster, shaped like volcanoes, covered the soggy beds and floors. Special lighting made it seem like flames were shooting out of the craters.

The third floor was "paradise." All the piled-up furniture made pathways for the guests. Soft green fabric covered the floors. Netting covered all the wet plaster, and fresh flowers were everywhere.

While the 500 guests, most in costumes, took the tour, servants transformed the main floor into a ballroom. Spanish moss and bats were the main decorations. Once all had gathered in the great hall, Lettie spoke to her guests. She thanked all those who helped during the night of the fire. Then the orchestra tuned up and the dancing began. There was food throughout the night, and the dancing stopped only at the first light of dawn.

Lettie, in her mischievous way, was thrilled at the success of the ball. She confided in her daughter, "There will never be another Halloween party like it. But the best part of all is that I rid my life of a whole lot of goblins."

Lettie continued to run her household, host parties, manage her business affairs, and devote much of her time to charitable causes. During World War I, she worked tirelessly for the Red Cross as head of the Flathead County Chapter. She was known across the state for her work.

Then, on a Sunday morning in June 1923, Lettie died quite unexpectedly in her beautiful house on Conrad Hill. The family held her funeral at the mansion. The home that she loved so much was full of her friends for the last time on that day. There was such a crowd that people had to stand on the lawn during the service. All the businesses in Kalispell closed for the funeral. A blanket of Lettie's favorite yellow flowers covered her casket. The hearse carrying her coffin traveled over flower petals that covered the driveway and the route to the cemetery.

As the years went by, vines and brambles grew over the walls of the mansion. The heat and the plumbing no longer worked. The roof leaked, and the ceiling plaster began to fall into the rooms. The house looked as bad as it had in 1910 after the fire.

Kalispell schoolchildren began to whisper about the house. There were so many weeds and brambles that you could hardly see the house from the street. Local children, and even some of their parents, were convinced that the old tumbledown mansion was haunted. It certainly *looked* like it was haunted. Some reported seeing people in the windows, peering out. Even to this day, visitors sometimes see faces at the windows. Could these be the spirits of the Conrad family, watching over the house? Or long-dead guests who enjoyed Lettie's gracious hospitality?

In the early 1970s, Lettie's daughter Alicia gave the mansion and everything inside to the City of Kalispell. The mansion was full of furniture, boxes, and personal belongings. There were clothes in the closets and dishes in the cupboards. The house, however, needed a lot of work. Many people, including Alicia, wanted the city to turn the mansion into a museum.

Restoration of the mansion took a long time. Many people gave money and time to help fix it up. In the 1980s, Arvid "Kris" Kristoffersen did all the inside painting. Kris is an artist and a "color detective." He carefully went over every room to find its original color. He took down fixtures to find traces of the original paint. Then he painted the walls and woodwork of each room, one by one. While he was working on this long project, he had two eerie experiences.

Late one afternoon, Kris was alone in a second-floor bedroom when he heard footsteps in the quiet house. "You can tell whether footsteps are male or female," he says. "These were female."

He heard someone coming down the hallway and looked up to see a figure pass by. It was a slightly heavyset woman in a white, ankle-length dress and black boots with fancy laces. Kris went to the doorway and watched the figure disappear down the stairs. After the woman was out of sight, he heard her footsteps fade into the kitchen.

A few days after the first incident, Kris and his partner were working downstairs in the music room doorway, alone in the house. It was very quiet. A noise at the top of the stairs caught their attention. Looking up, they both could see the rocking chair in its usual place at the head of the stairs. But in the still of this quiet afternoon, it was moving back and forth, back and forth. The two men gathered their paintbrushes and called it a day. In retrospect, Kris feels sure that, on both occasions, Lettie Conrad paid them a visit to say she found their work satisfactory.

Some months later, museum employees were going through the clothing in an upstairs closet. They found a very old, ankle-length white dress. They called Kris over to look at it. Sure enough, it was same dress worn by the ghostly woman in the hallway.

Lettie always knew how to show her guests a good time. Today, the beautiful mansion is again a home to be proud of. And Lettie, ever the gracious hostess, still welcomes her visitors.

Chapter Ten
The Mansion's Little Ghost

THE LITTLE BLACK CAT WITH THE SLEEK COAT CREPT UP THE back stairs, along the hallway, and into the children's playroom. Looking for company, it quietly walked past the seamstress's dress form and sewing machine. The cat sniffed the dolls in the cradle, stretched on the rag rug, rubbed up against the corner of the dollhouse, and disappeared…

If walls could talk, the Original Governor's Mansion in Helena would have a lot to say. Three private families and nine governors have lived in the large brick home. Its past residents have left their stories behind. Some of them have left more than just stories.

In 1887, the Chessman family built the stylish, twenty-room home in Helena. The mansion has a grand oak staircase, many nooks and crannies, turrets, balconies, and a ballroom. The Chessmans lived in the home for about thirteen years before they sold it and moved out.

From 1913 to 1959, the mansion was home to the families of nine Montana governors. The three Stewart girls, whose father was Governor Samuel Stewart, were the first of the governors' children to move to the mansion in 1913. The girls fell in love with their new home. The nooks and crannies were perfect for games of hide-and-seek, but the ballroom on the third floor became their special playroom. The Stewart girls kept their dolls and treasures there and played with their friends. When the visiting seamstress would come to make their new clothes, she worked in the play-room. There was a dress form she used like a mannequin to fit the clothing. The Stewart girls and the other governors' children after them kept the upper floors full of laughter and mischief.

By 1959, however, the mansion's elegance had faded. A new governor's home was built across town. Dark and shuttered, the old mansion sat quiet and empty. For several years during the 1960s, a caretaker lived at the mansion. She would often answer the doorbell and find children of the former governors, all grown up, standing on the porch. She would invite them in and let them poke around in the unused rooms and listen to their stories about living in the mansion.

From these visitors, she heard two stories that startled her. Children who had lived in the mansion at different times—and who had never met—all saw the same strange things.

Many of the children who lived in the mansion remembered being terrified of something they all called the "It." The It lived in the upstairs hallway. When the grown-up children talked about this scary thing that hid on the second floor, their grown-up voices grew quiet. It seemed painful for them to talk about the incidents. But the caretaker heard the tale time and again. It was always the same.

"There was a door upstairs in the hallway," they would start out. "This door was very hard to open. But the It, who lived in the house, could always open the door without making a sound."

The camera captured an odd mist, upper right center, in this 1913 photo of the reception hall in the Original Governor's Mansion in Helena. Could this be the It?
PHOTO COURTESY OF THE MONTANA HISTORICAL SOCIETY RESEARCH CENTER.

The children would test the It by shutting the door tightly when they went to bed. In the morning, the door would always be standing open. The children shivered in their beds at night, wondering if the It was lurking in the hallway outside their doors.

Several generations of tour guides have spent time alone in the mansion in the last thirty years. Today, they sometimes find shades pulled up when they were left down. Small things might be out of place. A picture, for example, might be turned to the wall. Or a closet door that is always kept shut might be discovered wide open.

One morning recently, a newly hired guide unlocked the front door and stepped inside to find a fan running. No one had been in the mansion since he locked the door the day before. He clearly remembered turning the fan off at the end of the previous day. He went to check the third-floor fan. It was off as he had left it, but someone, or *something*, had turned the dress form in the children's room almost completely around. Could these incidents be the result of the It, still up to mischief?

The second story the caretaker heard from many of the former governors' now grown-up children was about a little cat. This little cat roamed the mansion's hallways. It was a friendly little kitty, and it always came to them, begging for attention, its long tail held high, straight up in the air. Time and again, the lucky child who had the cat's attention would bend down to scoop it up. But just as the child's hands were about to close over the sleek little body, the ghost cat would disappear.

Why would a ghostly cat appear in the mansion? Researchers found an interesting photograph in the Montana Historical

Society archives. It shows the Chessmans, who built the home, with a professional photographer taking a portrait of the family's sleek black cat!

Why do you think the little cat ghost has disappeared? Perhaps it takes a family, or someone like you, to conjure him back into the halls of the mansion. Now that you know this secret, if you visit the historic home, you might coax him out of hiding. Look sharp and open your heart. Maybe you can make friends with the mansion's smallest ghost.

The Chessman family hired a photographer to take pictures of their beloved cat outside their home, now the Original Governor's Mansion, in Helena.
PHOTO COURTESY OF THE MONTANA HISTORICAL SOCIETY RESEARCH CENTER.

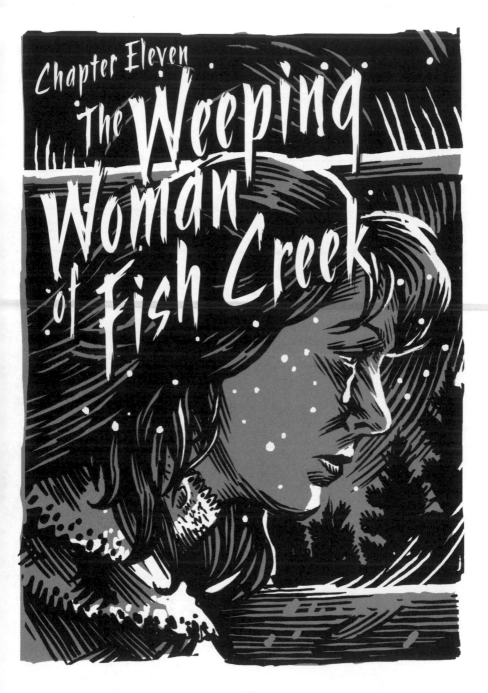

Chapter Eleven

The Weeping Woman of Fish Creek

Up on a lonely hillside, not far from Missoula, an abandoned cabin once sat nestled against the slope. Fallen trees—with branches that looked like the arms of skeletons reaching out from the grave—surrounded it. But the cabin's appearance was not nearly as scary as what haunted it.

It seems like the cabin was always in a sagging state. Long ago, railroad crews would stop in the area to rest, and they'd camp out in the old building. Hunters also discovered the abandoned homestead. They, too, curled up in their blankets to get a few hours' rest. There was good fishing in nearby Fish Creek, and so fishermen used the old house as a home base.

Years went by, and the house remained. Its walls weakened and its logs sagged, but that old house hugged the hillside, not wanting to let go.

Over time, the old homestead developed a reputation. People saw something there, and it scared them. Many believed a ghost lived in the cabin.

One Saturday night in January 1915, three railroad men decided to investigate. So they got off the train at the tiny town of Rivulet, climbed up the steep path to the mysterious cabin, and stepped inside.

Far into the night they kept one another awake, telling stories and waiting for the ghost to appear. They had heard that ghosts were supposed to appear at midnight. When the spook didn't show up, the men figured they'd turn in for the night. They spread their blankets on the cracked floorboards and fell asleep. One snored softly. Another smiled as he dreamed of his

warm bed at home. The third man slept more deeply than the other two. The wind whistled through the broken windows, and moonlight made little pools beneath them.

A peculiar moan startled one of the sleepers. His soft snore became a snort as he struggled to awaken at the odd sound. He sat up, throwing his blanket aside even though the January night was cold. He listened intently. There it was again.

The man nudged one of his companions. Grumbling and turning over, the second man opened his eyes.

"Come on, man! Wake up!" the first man hissed.

His friend groaned and sat up. "What's going on?" he asked groggily.

The first man pointed. He saw a woman, dressed in a silk bridal gown. She came out of the bedroom and stood in the doorway. She was crying. The woman then crossed the room and moved to the window, her silk dress fluttering. Its sheen caught the moonlight. Then she disappeared.

The second man saw something different. He saw only a face in the darkness. It was the sorrowful face of a woman, with tearful, staring eyes, floating in the doorway. If there was a body attached, he did not see it. He blinked and she was gone.

The two men sat motionless. They heard the wind rise and fall in the trees outside. They peered into the darkness, wondering if the weeping woman would return. The men listened intently. Nothing moved, and the third man continued to sleep deeply. When faint sunlight appeared on the horizon, they awakened the third man, packed their gear, and climbed down to Rivulet in time to catch their train.

Word of the men's encounter with "the weeping woman" quickly spread. Others stepped forward, claiming they, too, had seen the weeping woman. Some saw the ghost on the hillside. Others saw her inside the cabin, and still others saw her roaming along the railroad tracks. The ghost appeared differently to different people. But there was one thing all the sightings had in common: the ghost was always crying.

In January and February of 1915, the number of sightings grew. The famous Weeping Woman of Fish Creek even appeared to reporters and photographers from the *Missoulian* newspaper. Around three in the morning, they awoke and glimpsed the weeping woman. She was standing at the edge of the forest in the moonlight, wringing her hands and crying pitifully.

Stories of the Weeping Woman of Fish Creek have been told for generations. Children in the Missoula area grew up hearing stories about the ghostly woman. When Cheryl Stewart was growing up in eastern Montana, her family spent part of the summer with her mother's family in western Montana. They heard the stories about the haunted cabin above Rivulet from their Uncle Ray.

Uncle Ray was a highway patrolman. He told the kids that once, when he was out on patrol in the Fish Creek area, a mysterious force grabbed his steering wheel and tried to force him off the old dirt road. He refused to go near the place after that.

The kids begged Uncle Ray to take them out to the old dirt road that led to the haunted cabin, but he always said no. Finally, one summer, the kids persuaded him to drive the sixty miles out to Fish Creek. "Maybe we can catch a glimpse of the Weeping

Woman of Fish Creek," said Uncle Ray mysteriously. Cheryl and her brothers and cousins could hardly wait.

The moon was full and tensions rose in the car as they got closer to the turn-off. They turned off the highway onto the dirt road at the old railway stop. No trains stopped there anymore, and the tiny town of Rivulet no longer existed. They made their way along the road and soon came to an old sign that said "Fish Creek."

Suddenly Uncle Ray violently turned the steering wheel and the car swerved.

"What are you doing?" the kids all yelled at once.

"Something turned the wheel," said Uncle Ray. His voice shook, but the kids could not tell if he was really upset or if he was just kidding around.

They found themselves heading down a narrow road. It was so overgrown that the tall pines looming overhead hid the moonlight. Uncle Ray wanted to turn back, but the road was so narrow that they had no choice. They had to keep going. The headlights cast a lonely beam, paving their way.

The kids kept a lookout for signs of the ghost as Uncle Ray maneuvered the car down the winding, shadowy road. They were beginning to doubt his fantastic stories about the unseen force and the ghost of the weeping woman. The road finally widened, and they found themselves in a large, open meadow.

The moon lit the meadow with an eerie glow as Uncle Ray switched off the headlights.

"There! There! Look!" one of the cousins cried. The car filled with screams as Cheryl and the other kids hit the floor in terror. Just ahead of the car, Cheryl saw three white figures moving to and fro, dancing in the moonlight. Two of them were exactly alike, their white dresses fluttering in the breeze. But the third one looked a little grayer and seemed to glide, or *float*, over the moonlit meadow.

According to Cheryl, her brother Spence remembered another detail about that night and the meadow in the moonlight. As they saw the figures gliding through the meadow, Uncle Ray quickly turned the car around. For a moment, the headlights pointed to a hillside. Spence saw a huge ball of fire rushing down. It horrified him. He was afraid it would hit them. The ball of fire hurtled down the hill at lightning speed. Closer and closer it came. There was a blinding flash. The fireball must have gone right through the car. Then it disappeared.

All the way home, Cheryl, her brothers, and their cousins were silent as they drove down the moonlit highway. Once they were home, seated around the familiar kitchen table, they began to talk about what they had just seen. Cheryl's mother and aunt listened quietly to their story. The children were very scared and upset. They had wanted to see the weeping woman, but they did not really think they would. The children were so shaken that finally Cheryl's mother spoke up.

"Okay, okay. We can see that you guys are really scared. Your aunt and I have a confession to make," she said, pausing. Everyone stopped to listen. "What you saw up there was really just us, dressed up in some old sheets. We thought it would be a good joke!"

Cheryl, her brothers, and their cousins all began to talk at once. Finally, one of them spoke up louder than the others.

"So how many of you were up there?" asked one of the cousins.

"Why, just your mom and me. That's two of us," said Cheryl's mother.

But the kids looked stunned. "What do you mean, there were two of you?" they all cried at once.

"What are you talking about?" asked Cheryl's mom, not understanding the problem. "It was just the two of us, dancing in the meadow."

The room fell quiet. Uncle Ray finally turned and asked the kids, "How many figures did you guys see?"

All the children agreed that they had seen not two but *three* figures in the meadow, moving to and fro.

To this day, a tingle runs along Cheryl's spine when she recalls the third ghost, the one that looked a little grayer than the other two as it floated over the moonlit meadow.

*D*O YOU HAVE MIRRORS AT YOUR HOUSE? SOME PEOPLE believe that mirrors are portals, or doorways, to the supernatural. They say that spirits sometimes try to communicate through mirrors. Perhaps this explains the strange phenomena at Main Hall at the University of Montana, where custodians, students, and others have seen eerie reflections.

Main Hall is the oldest building on campus. Since the first students gathered there for classes in 1899, the bells in Main Hall's tower have kept time. They ring out over the campus every hour. Although the building's old wooden floors creak, its pipes are noisy, and its corners are musty, students enjoy its charm.

Generations of students have swapped ghost stories about campus buildings. They gather in the dorms when studying is finished and the hour grows late. Stories tend to begin with a thread of truth that almost always becomes frayed over time. Details change, and names are lost. Stories passed down over many years usually change quite a bit and have little truth left in them. It is only natural. When we become storytellers, we twist the truth to please our audiences. In this way, legend becomes fact, and truth takes a back seat.

For University of Montana graduate student David Dick, truth is more important than storytelling. He is interested in science, especially anthropology, which is the study of human societies and cultures. As he took classes in the various buildings, David heard snippets of old ghost stories. He heard about the ghostly German shepherd that some say roams the corridors of Brantly Hall. He also heard something about the noisy ghosts who fill a classroom in Rankin Hall after hours. He heard threads of stories about Main Hall, too. According to campus lore, the building has long been known for scaring the custodians who worked there at night. Reflections bounce off the many windows and mirrors, and the creaky floors and noisy pipes make you stop to listen for something more.

One story about Main Hall involves a custodian who was cleaning a sink in the women's restroom. His work was interrupted when he caught a glimpse of a dark-haired young woman. He saw her image in the mirror, and she appeared to be standing behind him! He whirled around, but there was no one there.

David had heard all the stories. But then, one day in the fall

Many people have reported seeing strange images in mirrors and ghostly figures in the halls of Main Hall on the University of Montana campus. PHOTO BY KATIE BAUMLER.

of 2006, he became part of one of the stories. David had a class on the third floor of Main Hall. It was early in the semester, and the class was full. He had a seat in the back row next to the door in the lecture hall. The professor was droning on. David quietly slipped out of his seat and headed down the several flights of stairs to the only men's room in the building, which was in the basement. He pushed the door open and stepped inside. Immediately, something about the room didn't feel right. He couldn't put his finger on it at first. Then he realized what it was. He had the distinct feeling that someone was watching him.

David did not like the feeling. He nervously stood at the sink and washed his hands. Then through the mirror above the sink, he saw a middle-aged man enter the bathroom, go into a stall, and shut the door. That seemed normal enough, but David still felt weird. There was a strange energy in the air, and David could not shake the feeling that someone was watching him.

David reached for the paper towels. The dispenser was stuck. As he wrestled with the machine, he began to wonder if the man was still in the stall. David had not seen the man come out. He had not heard a single sound. The room was eerily silent.

Finally, David turned away from the mirror and faced the stalls. Unlike how it appeared in the mirror, the stall door was not shut; it was slightly ajar. He saw no feet, heard no noise. David stepped toward the stall. He took a deep breath, carefully put his hand on the door, and gave it a hard, deliberate push. The door swung open wide, but no one was there.

David returned to his class on the third floor, slipped through the door, and quietly slid into his seat. He later told a friend about his experience in the men's room. The friend made little comment. He only remarked that the building was supposed to be haunted. Then David tried to forget about it.

Try as he might, David could not put the odd experience out of his mind. It kept coming back to haunt him. In thinking about what he saw, he recalled that there had been something strange about the man in the mirror. First, he somehow looked undefined or blurry at the edges. David saw him only from the waist up, but he remembered that the man wore a plaid flannel shirt and was in his forties or fifties. The other weird thing was that the image seemed to appear not directly behind him, but in the corner of the mirror.

David settled into his school routine. However, he could not forget the strange experience in Main Hall. Weeks went by. Around Halloween, David saw an article in the student newspaper. It was about local ghost hunters Erik and Kris Bratlien, who had recently spent a night at Main Hall. When David read about their investigations in the building, he shook his head. This was no coincidence.

The ghost hunters took several pictures inside the men's room where David saw the man in the mirror. They saw nothing unusual, so they closed the door and moved on. No one else was in the hallway. But later, when the group came back down the hall, the door to the men's room stood *open*.

David is a man of science—of logic and truth. But he has no explanation for what he saw that day, or how it relates to the dozens of other stories about Main Hall. Now, he never looks in a mirror without wondering what might appear behind him.

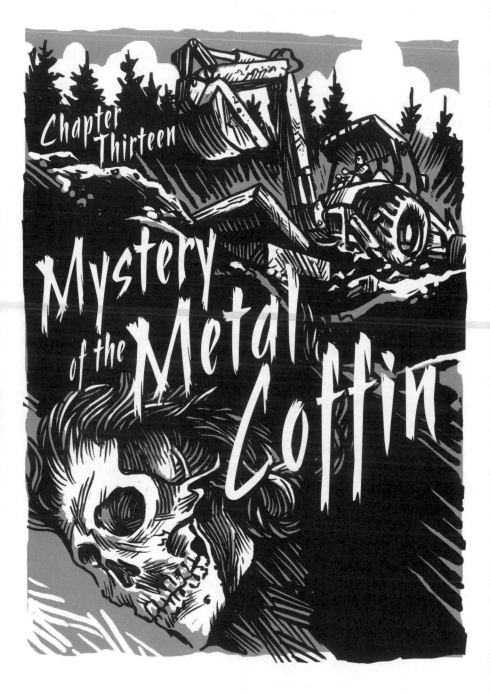

Chapter Thirteen

Mystery of the Metal Coffin

THUNK! THE BACKHOE'S METAL BUCKET STRUCK SOMETHING hard. A construction crew was digging a foundation for a new home at the Red Cliff Estates in the town of Clancy. Out of the corner of his eye, the backhoe operator saw an object roll free. It left a shiny, wet path like a snail, only much larger. The operator switched off the engine and jumped down to investigate. He was horrified to see that lying there, nestled against the sandy soil, was a human skull.

The hair was long and coiled into a bun. A chill ran along the operator's spine as his eyes followed the wet trail the skull had made. He saw that it had fallen out of a large cast-iron coffin— the object he hit with the backhoe. The casket had beautiful

A backhoe operator digging the foundation for a house in Clancy made a shocking discovery when he hit a metal casket and a skull rolled out.

PHOTO COURTESY OF CRAIG DOOLITTLE.

silver-plated handles and a "viewing" window—a piece of glass in the lid so that mourners could see the face of the person inside.

The backhoe's bucket had broken the glass, causing the skull to roll out. The casket itself was narrow at the bottom and wider at the shoulders, in the style of long ago. The man could see that the body—minus its head—no longer rested comfortably on the padded silk bed. It now lay jumbled inside its metal cocoon.

Whose grave was this? No one knew. The Haynes family, who owned the property all the way back to 1892, knew of no one who had been buried there. Sheriff Craig Doolittle took photographs of the grave and then moved the coffin to the Clancy cemetery. Meanwhile, Charleen Spalding, a woman with a knack for solving mysteries about cemeteries and people buried in them, took up the search to discover who this person was.

With the backhoe's grisly discovery, people began to tell stories about the ancient Red Cliff farmhouse. It stood just off the interstate, on North Main Street in Clancy. There was talk of a shadowy figure in an upstairs window, doors that open and close on their own, and footsteps in the attic.

Charleen discovered a story that began long ago…

Music drifted out of the open window of the white house in the tiny town of Clancy. It carried above the fields and filtered through the Red Cliff horse barn, over the heads of Silas Harvey's thoroughbred trotting horses. The song carried down the lane. The notes of the piano reached the ears of the men gathered at the bar behind Henry Hill's post office and general store.

*Silas Harvey built this farmhouse in Clancy where tenants have reported ghostly
activity. The Haynes family, pictured here, bought the farm in 1892.*
PHOTO COURTESY OF GWEN HAYNES HARTMAN.

"That's a sign of refinement," sighed the postmaster. "Clancy
is destined for great things." He shut his eyes and pictured the
Harvey home up the road, with Evelyn seated at her piano.

Evelyn Harvey's grand piano had come by train, steamboat,
and ox team all the way from New York. The piano, in its carved
rosewood cabinet, was the talk of the town. It had been a gift
from her father, Silas.

On this warm October afternoon in 1876, life was very good

for the Harvey family. Silas bred champion trotting horses at Red Cliff Farm. His best horse, Black Diamond, was his pride and joy. Diamond was coal black and very fast. He came all the way from Kentucky and won many races.

As the 1870s ended, however, life in the Harvey household took a turn when Silas became ill. At about the same time, a dark-haired young man named John Eddy began to visit Evelyn. John had a magnificent singing voice. The couple spent many hours together at the rosewood piano. The music they made together filled the Harvey home with warmth and eased Silas Harvey's last, painful days.

In the early morning of May 7, 1879, Silas Harvey took his last labored breath. The funeral service took place in the parlor, with Silas laid out in his coffin, dressed in his best suit. Someone played the rosewood piano for the simple service. Silas's passing left a deep impression on the rooms of the white house.

Evelyn and John married soon after Silas's death. But their happiness did not last. This was the beginning of a series of tragic events for the family. In just a few years, Evelyn, her daughter, and her grandmother all died. With an aching heart, Evelyn's mother, Frances Harvey, sold the prize stallions, mares, and colts and the bank took Red Cliff Farm. And Evelyn's piano—the source of so many happy memories—was sold.

Frances Harvey moved out of the white house, where the family knew much joy and much sadness. And the Harveys left their mark upon its rooms.

Through records and documents, Charleen pieced the Harvey family story together. She learned about four family members who died while the family lived in the white house at Red Cliff Farm: Silas Harvey, Evelyn Harvey Eddy, Evelyn's daughter Esta Clara, and Evelyn's grandmother Rebecca Addis. Did the mysterious coffin belong to one of these family members?

One puzzle piece led to another. The size of the coffin suggested the person was female. The long, coiled hair also suggested that the person was a woman. Scientists at the University of Montana who looked at Sheriff Doolittle's photographs agreed. One professor noticed something else: the person's nasal cavity was quite large. This suggested that she must have had a very unique and prominent nose. Charleen continued to gather information, investigating every lead. But she found no pictures of the Harvey women. No one could tell if one of these women had a large nose.

Meanwhile, the Boulder newspaper interviewed a woman named Patrice Payne Fritsch, who used to live at the Red Cliff Farm. She loved the old farmhouse, but she said some strange things happened while she lived there. One night Patrice's husband, Scott, was out late at a meeting, so she went to bed. A little later, Patrice heard footsteps. She thought it was her husband coming home, so she got up to meet him. But he was not there. Patrice sensed, however, that someone was in the room with her. She stood frozen, uncertain what to do. As she stood there in the semi-darkness, she clearly saw the edge of the bed sink, as if someone was sitting down.

There were other incidents, too. Patrice and her daughter came home late one night. As they approached the house, both could see a light in the attic. Patrice was sure she had not left the light on. They looked up to the window. There was someone standing there. The attic light behind the figure cast a perfect outline, but it was impossible to tell if the shadowy figure was gazing out over the field or *watching them.*

On another occasion, the sound of a door opening and shutting kept one of Patrice's daughters awake until she called out for it to stop, which it did. And on another day, visitors to the house witnessed the drawers in a dresser open and shut by themselves.

Charleen had collected a lot of records and other evidence, and she was pretty sure she had solved the mystery of the strange metal coffin. But still she wondered if she was right. So, on an afternoon in late October, as the leaves began to fall and a hint of cold weather blew a chill through the wind, she and several others gathered on the road beside the white house. Horses in the corral stared at the strangers. One sleek, dark beauty—reminiscent of the famed Black Diamond who once lived there so many generations ago—paced back and forth nervously.

One of the visitors gathered with Charleen was Shanda Sims, a lovely, enthusiastic young woman very sensitive to people, places, and their energies. Shanda knew about the discovery of the coffin, but she knew nothing about Red Cliff Farm or the Harvey family.

As the horses continued to stare and the dark one nervously paced, Shanda said some interesting things. She felt very strongly there had once been a headstone or pile of stones marking the grave. Shanda was certain that the person buried there was a woman, a younger woman, deeply mourned by her mother and

husband. She also sensed the burial of another person, a man, in the general area. Might this have been Silas Harvey, whose burial place is still a mystery? According to Shanda, these burial places had been carefully chosen so that, in eternal rest, the departed might observe what was happening on the land they had loved.

The wind, already strong, began to blow harder and colder; the group huddled together. The horses continued to stare, and the dark one paced back and forth. He seemed to be staring at the house. Shanda looked in that direction and gazed at the house for a few moments. Suddenly, she spoke.

"There is someone watching us from the attic window," Shanda said. "The person is gazing out over the field, very quietly. I sense utter sadness in this person, and the spirit of a small child is there, too." Was it Evelyn and her daughter Esta Clara?

Shanda closed her eyes and concentrated harder. Then she finally spoke again. "I clearly see a woman—the same woman who is in the casket. There is a man with dark hair—the same man who was so grief-stricken at her death. He is standing over her, and she is seated at a piano, playing."

Shanda continued to concentrate quietly, trying to see details. Then she opened her eyes wide and smiled as if she had just discovered a secret. She laughed a little. "Say," said Shanda. "The woman has something very distinctive about her. She has a very strong, large nose."

Index

Page numbers for photographs are in italics.

Horse Slaughter Camp 27
house of crying babies (Bannack) 67

I

Ives, George 12, *13*

J

James, Toni 43–44
Johnson, Nord 80

K

Kalispell ghosts 83–91
Kelley's Saloon (Garnet) 58
Kentucky Derby 28–31
Kim Newman 71–72
Kristoffersen, Arvid "Kris" 89–91

L

Lowe, Tom 70–71

M

Main Hall (University of Montana) 107–111, *109*
map of story locations *17*
Marsolek, Patrick 71
Martinka, Kathy 72
Mathews, Allan 61–62
Mathews, Bertie 67–68
Mathews, Montie 67
Mathews, Rufus 67
Meade, John S. 66
Meade, Louisa 66
Meade Hotel (Bannack) 66–67, 69–71, *73*
Mill, George G. 35

About the Author

Ellen Baumler is an award-winning author and the Montana Historical Society's interpretive historian. A master at linking history with modern-day supernatural events, Ellen has delighted audiences across the state with her true stories. She lives in Helena in a century-old house with her husband, Mark, and its resident spirits. *Montana Chillers* is her first book for younger readers.